ENDORSEMENTS

Randal D. Lewis,
Board Member / Management Consultant / CPG Executive

As the COO of Spectrum Brands, I watched how disciplined execution and a genuine focus on people turned the struggling Blacksburg facility into a flagship operation. *They Just Don't Get It* captures those same fundamentals—not as theory, but as a playbook forged in real plants with real results. Any leader serious about bridging the gap between strategy and execution will find tremendous value here.

John Stock
Retired Senior Director of Manufacturing Operations

I spent 42 years in manufacturing and experienced most of the challenges described in this book. Early on, when I was a line supervisor, I was valued as a good firefighter. As my career advanced, I learned that real progress comes from slowing down, listening to people, and respecting the process. That's exactly what this book reinforces. There's a wealth of practical wisdom here for leaders at every level—insights that are as useful as anything you'd find in a graduate course but grounded in real-world experience.

Jay Foster
Founder of Flex-Metrics

After nearly three decades building Flex-Metrics, I've seen many leaders use the platform. Don Robb stands apart in how he transforms data into action. This book captures the essence of leadership that doesn't just monitor performance—it empowers teams to take ownership, drive meaningful change, and unlock potential. A must-read for anyone serious about leading a plant to operational excellence and bottom-line results.

Mike Flint
Former Director, Center for Business Analytics, Virginia Tech Businessman, Entrepreneur, Investor, Board Member, "Data Disciple"

Spoken with decades of manufacturing experience, Don Robb and Bob Siepka show how data can transform the shop floor into a PRODUCTION POWERHOUSE! But this book is not just for manufacturing leaders; all business leaders can learn the value data provides our companies--in understanding our business, identifying and solving problems, selling solutions, and serving our most critical constituents: our customers!

Jon Casto
Managing Director | Supply Chain & Network Ecosystem Strategy, Engineering, and Execution

They Just Don't Get It isn't theory—I saw it in action during the Roanoke plant turnaround. When trust, data-driven leadership, and alignment merge, breakthrough results follow. The universal principles in this book became my compass, carrying me from manufacturing leadership to global logistics and supply chain consulting. They remain a timeless guide for any leader seeking to bridge strategy and execution and deliver lasting success.

Michelle Jones
Chief Financial Officer, Rowe Furniture

As the finance partner who worked side by side with the Spectrum Brands team during that turnaround, I can say with certainty that every principle in this book works. *They Just Don't Get It* perfectly captures the tension and opportunity that exists between strategy and execution along with the vital role of the middle leaders who make things happen. From the finance seat, I saw firsthand how clarity, trust, and disciplined follow-through turn abstract strategy into measurable success. This book is not theory; it's lived experience. The insights will resonate with anyone who's ever been the bridge between vision and results and remind every leader that alignment, accountability, and empathy are what truly drive performance.

Don Robb with Bob Siepka

Contributions by Ben Velker

Foreward by Jack Stack
author of
The Great Game of Business

They Just Don't Get It!

How Manufacturing Site
Leaders Translate Between
Strategy & Execution

They Just Don't Get It!
© 2025 SoftSolutions Inc.
All rights reserved.

ISBN: 979-8-9933245-0-0
Library of Congress Control Number: Pending

Edited by **Ben Velker** and **Jennifer May**
Design by **Ben Velker**

First Edition
Printed in the United States of America

Publisher:
SoftSolutions Inc.
www.flex-metrics.com

ACKNOWLEDGEMENTS:

THE TURTLE ON THE FENCE POST

There's an old saying: "If you ever see a turtle on a fence post, you know one thing for sure—it didn't get there by itself."

Whatever success we've had as leaders came from being lifted by others—leaders, mentors, and colleagues who guided and challenged us, friends and family who supported us, and, most of all, the teams we worked with.

Those teams pushed us to be better leaders. Great followers don't just get the job done—they shape the leaders they choose to follow. To every person who walked this road with us: thank you.

We want to thank Jack Stack for his generous contribution to this book. His words lend immediate weight and credibility—but even more importantly, the concepts we learned from him profoundly shaped our own leadership journey. Jack's insights into open-book management and practical leadership have guided how we think, how we lead, and how we strive to bridge the gap between executives and the shop floor. This book stands on the foundation of those lessons.

A special thanks to Ben Velker. This book wouldn't exist without his gentle push and unwavering belief that it could be done. He spent hours interviewing us, drawing out our stories and ideas, and then turned those conversations into the very first outline of this book. More than a collaborator, Ben was a friend who gave us the momentum to get started and the confidence to keep going.

And to Dr. Tracy Wilkins—scientist, entrepreneur, friend, mentor, and the driving force behind Flex-Metrics. Tracy has a way of seeing not just what we're doing, but why it matters, and he never let us settle for keeping our story to ourselves. He pushed, prodded, and reminded us that the lessons we've lived through could help others, and that leaving them untold would be a missed opportunity. When we resisted, he began to wonder if maybe we just didn't get it. This book exists in large part because of his persistence, vision, and belief that our experience was worth sharing.

FOREWORD BY JACK STACK

I admit I'm biased toward manufacturing---it's in my blood. My father worked in heavy manufacturing for more than thirty-five years, and I've been part of it myself since November of 1968.

My father had a significant influence on me because he was a measurement guy. He was a time study engineer, a cost accountant, and eventually ran a major welding organization before moving into supply chain. He measured everything---poker, horse racing, even my on-base percentage when I played baseball.

That focus on measurement shaped my life. Numbers have always guided me, and they ultimately carried me into the CEO chair, where I came to understand the financial ratios of business.

In my 50 years in manufacturing, I watched its contribution to GDP decline---until recently. Today, there's renewed conversation about making manufacturing great again. We're talking about the need to make things, to rebuild a rising middle class, to become more independent.

But the critical questions remain: Do we have the talent? Do we have the skill sets? Do we have the energy to support such a big, hairy, audacious goal?

That's why this book, They Just Don't Get It by Don Robb and Bob Siepka, matters. It's the first book on manufacturing I've seen since Edward Deming was elevated to sainthood! It's a fresh start, breaking down the language of manufacturing to reveal its hidden benefits and the power you gain when you truly get it.

At SRC, we learned this lesson the hard way. When we bought our failing plant from International Harvester in 1983, we couldn't rely on traditional ways of managing because they wouldn't produce the kind of results we needed in time to save us. So, we grabbed for something new, based on what we thought of as the higher laws of business.

THE FIRST HIGHER LAW IS: You Get What You Give. THE SECOND HIGHER LAW IS: It's Easy to Stop One Guy, But It's Pretty Hard to Stop 100. These weren't theories from business school—they were street-smart principles forged on the factory floor by people fighting for their jobs.

What Don and Bob understand—and what this book captures—is that the best, most efficient, most profitable way to operate a business is to give everybody in the company a voice in how the work gets done and a clear understanding of how their efforts drive business results. But here's the key: you can't just give people a voice. You have to teach them the language of business first.

That's exactly what site leaders do every day. They stand in the middle, translating between two worlds—turning executive strategy into shop floor action, and shop floor reality into business results. They're the ones who make the connection between daily work and financial impact visible to everyone.

When we first introduced The Great Game of Business, we said the key was to teach the rules, follow the action, and deliver a stake in the outcome. This book picks up that torch and shows how site leaders can bring those principles to life every day—not just in times of crisis, but as a way of operating that builds capability and drives results.

As I often say, "If they knew what we know, they'd make better decisions." Don and Bob's book is about making sure they do know—and that starts with leaders who can bridge the gap.

Read They Just Don't Get It and unleash the power of understanding both the language of manufacturing and the language of business. These metrics are stories about people. Learn their meanings and practices, and you'll not only change your thinking forever—you'll know how to play to win.

JACK STACK
CEO, SRC Holdings Corporation

PREFACE

THE PROMISE AND CHALLENGE TO THE SITE LEADER

As a site manufacturing leader, you're on a journey that demands constant translation—turning strategy into execution, intent into outcome.

Sometimes you're a megaphone, amplifying corporate direction so your teams understand what's expected. Other times you're a translator, converting objectives into priorities and actions that make sense on the shop floor. But always, you are a leader—and leadership is influence.

Your role exists for a clear reason: to deliver the results the company expects. You do that not by choosing sides but by connecting them—aligning strategy and execution, people and process, intent and outcome.

It often feels like you're caught in the middle—between the demands from above and the realities below. At times it's a game of corporate keep-away, where resources and clarity never quite reach you; other times it's shopfloor keep-away, where you can't get a straight read on what's really happening. The noise and motion can leave you feeling trapped in chaos.

You can't survive there. Leaders step back far enough to see the big picture—to connect the dots, identify what truly matters, and bring clarity to the noise.

Here's an uncomfortable truth: executives usually don't get it—and it isn't really their job to. Their focus is shareholder value and strategy. Most people on the floor don't get it either—because no one's ever shown them how their work connects to that bigger picture.

That's the gap between strategy and reality. And that's where you live.

You can stop being the victim stuck between two worlds. You can stop feeling caught between those who expect results and those who make them happen. You can stop blaming leadership for being out of touch and stop assuming your workforce is uncommitted. Most people—on both sides—want to be part of something meaningful. They just need someone to show them how.

The pages that follow are built around real stories—moments from the plant floor and the executive suite where leadership lessons revealed themselves in unexpected ways. We invite you into those stories, not as an observer but as a fellow traveler. You'll see what we saw, feel the pressures we felt, and, we hope, discover the same principles that shaped the way we lead today.

This book helps you become that leader—not through heroics or firefighting, but through disciplined systems that build alignment and capability. You'll learn to:

Use data as your universal language—not spreadsheets, but visible, real-time information that gives everyone line of sight.

Find and tell the story in the data so that numbers move people, not just reports.

Develop the discipline to say no, distinguishing activity from impact.

Build ROI thinking into your DNA, shifting from cost center to profit center.

Unleash supervisors, managers, and partners, turning them from duct tape into multipliers.

Create culture you can see—where pride, trust, and purpose show up in behavior, not posters.

And you'll avoid three traps that keep site leaders stuck:

Stop being the **Hero** who relies on last-minute saves.

Stop being the **Veteran** with all the answers.

Stop being the **Fighter** who carries it alone.

Instead, become the **Builder**—a leader who constructs bridges, develops people, and leaves capability that outlasts them.

Every person in your organization rides the same bus. They need you—the one in the middle—to give them voice through data, purpose through connection, and pride through results.

Your executives are counting on performance.

Your employees are counting on leadership.

Your customers are counting on excellence.

They're all counting on you to make it work.

Are you ready to lead from the middle? Let's go.

INTRODUCTION:

CAUGHT IN THE MIDDLE

This isn't a typical business book written by MBAs or consultants parachuting in with theories and frameworks straight from the classroom or the latest best-seller.

It's built on more than seventy years of combined real-world manufacturing leadership—leading plants, turning around struggling operations, and working side by side with executives and shop-floor teams. We've seen what works, what doesn't, and how the gap between senior leaders and employees can either drive a business forward or drag it down.

You'll read lots of stories in this book, but very few of them are about colossal failures. We didn't learn our lessons by recovering from disaster—we learned them the way most site leaders do: through trial and error, through the daily grind of continuous improvement, by testing, adapting, and refining until the principles became clear. None of it came from theory; it came from doing the work, seeing what stuck, and learning from what didn't. That's why the stories in this book aren't about dramatic comebacks—they're about the steady, day-to-day discipline of getting better.

Along the way, we became aware of a common refrain—one we heard in conversations at every level of the organization. It became the title of this book.

How often have you heard someone say—or maybe you've said it yourself — "They just don't get it"?

It's whispered on the shop floor, where employees are convinced that executives don't understand—or care about—their reality.

It's spoken in the boardroom, where corporate leaders struggle to understand why operations can't execute.

This disconnect isn't usually about incompetence or arrogance. It's about different pressures, priorities, and languages.

Executives focus on strategy, growth, and profitability. They speak in terms of EBITDA, margins, market share, and shareholder value. Most have never worked on the floor, so they don't know what really happens day to day. Even the few who came up through operations aren't immune from the common refrain: "He used to be one of us, but he forgot everything he knew the moment he got promoted."

Meanwhile, the shop floor lives in a different world. Most employees have never heard corporate-speak in the first place. Their focus is the immediate: keeping machines running, meeting schedules, watching out for safety, solving quality problems, and simply getting through the shift. Strategy feels distant when you're living in a world where everything is both urgent and important.

That's why this book is written for site leaders—the ones caught in the middle. Their ultimate job description is simple: execute and deliver results. Fail at that, and you won't be in the role very long.

But delivering results isn't simple, because site leaders serve multiple masters. They must meet the demands of growth and profitability that drive shareholder value, while also dealing with the realities of the shop floor and the people who live it every day. At the same time, they need to earn trust, set expectations, inspire, and equip both sides to succeed. They must learn to lead in both directions.

The chapters that follow are built on real stories drawn from our own experience—stories from the plant floor and the executive suite. These aren't case studies polished after the fact; they're moments when alignment broke down and when it came back together.

When you see "I" or "we" in the stories, know that it's one of us speaking directly from experience.

Just Run Your Machines Faster!

It was peak season, and the plant had been oversold by 30%. The backlog was growing. Overtime was mandatory. Morale was crashing.

Despite heroic efforts—working weekends, optimizing production, pushing productivity—the team was still missing customer commitments.

Meanwhile, pressure was mounting. Customers were angry. Competitors were waiting in the wings with lower prices and promises of better service and delivery.

Leaders at the highest level demanded answers: why wasn't the plant delivering?

The call came: "Come to headquarters. The Executive Vice President wants to meet."

I walked into the boardroom, and I wasn't the only site leader on the firing line. One by one, my peers stood at the front of the room, delivering their presentations to the EVP. Each time, the pattern repeated: tough questions, sharp criticism, and no mercy. Charts were dismissed, assumptions shredded, excuses cut off mid-sentence. I sat and watched anxiously as my colleagues were eviscerated, fully aware that my turn was coming next.

But my presentation was cut short with one question: "Why can't you run your machines 30% faster?"

It sounded like he just didn't get it.

Arguing was clearly not an option. I simply said, "That's not possible—but we will find a way to increase output. I'll need your support."

Back at the plant, I gathered my leadership team and laid out the challenge. We collaborated to develop a plan to unite the workforce, explain the situation clearly, and set production targets that would dig us out of the hole. There was no time for new equipment or process upgrades—this would have to be pure discretionary effort and brute force.

Using principles from Jack Stack's The Great Game of Business, we designed a "small game" to reward employees for hitting the "critical number"—production targets that supported schedule-attainment goals.

The team rallied. They worked smarter, pushed harder, and found a way to deliver on commitments.

The lesson: when leaders from different worlds stop talking past each other and start working together, the magic happens. The executives got their results. The plant got the support it needed. And the employees got clarity on why their effort mattered.

Customers feel the impact of alignment just as much as executives or employees do. Missed shipments, poor quality, and broken promises erode trust faster than any metric on a scorecard. But when leaders connect people to purpose, employees respond with pride—and customers can see the difference.

We've watched it happen over and over again: happy employees create happy customers. And happy customers are the foundation of long-term success.

AUTHORS' NOTE

The story you just read isn't an isolated example. It captures the everyday reality of site leaders who live in the middle---pulled between corporate expectations and shop floor execution. This book is about giving those leaders a way forward: practical tools, a common language, and a framework for creating alignment---between strategy and execution, executives and employees, the top floor and the shop floor.

Between us, we've spent more than seventy years leading manufacturing operations. We're not consultants writing from the outside looking in---we've lived this work from the inside out.

At Flex-Metrics, we've had the privilege of working with dozens of manufacturing sites as they implemented data-driven improvement systems. Several stories in this book come from those partnerships, where we witnessed these principles in action across diverse industries and operating environments.

If you'd like more about backgrounds, see our bios and some case studies starting on page 157.

Our experiences---sometimes painful, sometimes transformative---taught us what it really takes to stand in the middle between executives and the shop floor. We've both seen strategies fall flat when they don't connect with reality, and we've seen plants come alive when leaders earn trust, make data visible, and align people with purpose. This book is our attempt to pass on those lessons in a way that's practical, honest, and field-tested.

To make it easier to follow, we've laid out a roadmap for the book. Think of it as a guided tour. Each chapter builds on the last, showing how site leaders move from seeing problems clearly to creating results that stick.

A ROADMAP FOR THE JOURNEY

The story "Just Run Your Machines Faster!" introduced the thread that runs through this book—the site leader's ongoing challenge of translating strategy into execution. It's the journey of leading from the middle: taking direction from above, turning it into action below, and using the tools at your disposal—your people, your processes, your equipment, and your access to corporate resources—to deliver results that last.

That thread connects every chapter that follows. Each part of the book builds on the last, guiding you from awareness to action, from execution to culture, and from individual leadership to organizational alignment. When that alignment happens, it doesn't just improve performance—it changes how customers experience your business. Engaged teams build trust inside the plant, and that trust becomes visible outside it.

Part I: The Current Reality

Before you can lead from the middle, you have to see clearly. This section focuses on awareness—understanding where you stand today, what your culture reveals, and what it hides.

Chapter 1 – U.S. Manufacturing at a Crossroads examines the real headwinds facing today's operations: a shrinking workforce, the loss of experience, and the need for leaders who can attract, develop, and retain talent. It begins with a fundamental truth every site leader eventually learns—we need the employees much more than they need us.

Chapter 2 – A Cultural Pulse Check helps you look at your plant with fresh eyes—through safety, housekeeping, and the everyday behaviors that tell you whether people take pride in their work or simply tolerate it.

This part gives you the perspective to diagnose your operation honestly. When leaders start seeing clearly, employees notice—and that attention to detail becomes the foundation of pride, quality, and the customer's trust in your product.

Part II: Delivering Results

Once you can see clearly, the next step is to connect what you see to what you do. This section moves from awareness to execution—the practical work of translating data into insight, insight into focus, and focus into measurable results.

Anchored by the bridge story "Feverishly Fighting to Exceed Our KPIs Every Hour of Every Day…", these chapters outline five levels of improvement—from quick fixes that fade to structural changes that define culture.

Chapter 3 – Data: The Foundation for Everything explores how reliable data becomes the currency of trust and the universal language of leadership.

Chapter 4 – Find the Story in the Data shows how to turn numbers into meaning—helping executives see value and employees see purpose.

Chapter 5 – You Can't Do Everything teaches the discipline of prioritization and the courage to say no.

Chapter 6 – The ROI of Fixing Problems reframes improvement as value creation—how to convert chronic issues into measurable business outcomes.

This part gives you the tools to translate expectations into results and to build credibility on both sides of the gap. As execution improves, customers begin to experience the difference—more reliability, better quality, and a sense that your organization simply delivers.

Part III: Leading Through People

At the heart of every operation are the people who make it run. This section focuses on leadership, culture, and influence—how to lead through others when you can't do it all yourself.

This part brings the journey full circle: from data to decisions, from systems to people, from compliance to commitment. When leaders invest in people, people invest in the work—and customers can feel that difference. Engaged teams take pride in what they produce, and that pride shows up in every shipment, every order, and every interaction.

The final section ties the thread together. The site leader's role is not just to deliver numbers but to build alignment—connecting executives and employees in a way that makes performance sustainable. When people understand the purpose behind the work, they deliver not only results but experiences that strengthen customer relationships.

Throughout this book, you'll notice the same thread woven through every story and principle:

Lead from the middle. See clearly. Translate effectively. Connect people to purpose. Deliver results that customers can feel.

That's the journey ahead. Let's begin.

PART I

THE CURRENT REALITY

CHAPTER 1:

U.S. MANUFACTURING AT A CROSSROADS

The leadership challenge that will define the next decade

Manufacturing is experiencing a moment of opportunity unlike any we've seen in decades. Supply chain disruptions exposed our over-dependence on foreign production. Companies are announcing massive investments to bring manufacturing home. Communities are competing for these new facilities, knowing they represent thousands of good-paying jobs and economic revitalization.

But there's a harsh reality beneath the optimism: we're trying to rebuild an industry while the workforce that built it is disappearing.

The Numbers Tell a Stark Story

The workforce crisis isn't speculation—it's already here, and it's accelerating:

- By 2033, nearly 2 million manufacturing jobs could go unfilled as 3.8 million positions open but only half can be filled with qualified workers.
- Every single day through 2027, over 11,000 Americans turn 65, creating a quarter-million job openings monthly across all industries. Manufacturing alone will lose 1.8 million workers to retirement—nearly 12% of the current workforce.
- The cost is staggering: Unfilled positions could cost the economy $1 trillion by 2030. Even when positions are filled, replacing a single skilled manufacturing worker costs between $10,000 and $40,000.

The math is brutal and simple: experienced workers are retiring faster than we can train replacements. And they're taking decades of institutional knowledge with them—knowledge about how machines really run, what problems look like before they become crises, and how to solve issues that aren't in any manual.

But even if we could replace them numerically, we'd still face a deeper problem.

The Cultural Disconnect

The challenge isn't just numerical. Today's manufacturing jobs are approaching 6 figures in total compensation (wages, benefits, bonuses), yet younger workers increasingly view the industry as outdated or unappealing. Meanwhile, the generation that built modern manufacturing—the Baby Boomers—is walking out the door en masse.

Today's workforce expects transparency, purpose, and respect. They want to understand the "why" behind their work, not just follow orders. They value work-life balance over unlimited overtime. They expect feedback, growth opportunities, and leaders who listen.

Traditional manufacturing leadership—built on hierarchy, secrecy, and "because I said so" authority—simply won't attract or retain the talent we need.

Somewhere along the line, we realized a truth that changed how we led: we need the employees much more than they need us. Without their skill, creativity, and commitment, no amount of strategy, technology, or capital investment will ever deliver results. That realization shaped everything about our leadership approach.

The companies that thrive in this new reality will be those that learn to lead differently. They'll create cultures of engagement rather than compliance. They'll treat employees as partners in solving problems, not just pairs of hands executing tasks. They'll build trust through transparency and earn commitment through clear purpose.

This isn't about being "soft" or lowering standards. It's about understanding that sustainable performance requires sustainable engagement. And engagement starts with leadership that bridges worlds—connecting business objectives with human motivation, strategic vision with daily reality.

Here's What That New Leadership Looks Like

The Spectrum Brands plant in Blacksburg, Virginia, once carried a terrible reputation. In the community, it was known as a dark, dirty, and difficult place to work. Inside the company, it wasn't regarded much better. Recruiting was an uphill battle, turnover was high, and morale was low.

I joined the Spectrum team as the Blacksburg plant manager during a company transition that led to the removal of the entire site leadership team. My first task was to build a new team from scratch (you'll read more about this crew in chapter 8). Then, we embarked on a journey to turn that ship around.

Our immediate priority was safety—every employee's well-being mattered more than production numbers, full stop. The second priority was simple but powerful: clean the place up. Housekeeping became a daily discipline. Locker rooms were cleaned and painted. Break rooms were restocked and refreshed.

Next, we re-energized the shop floor data system, not as a reporting tool but as a problem-solving engine. By using data to pinpoint real issues that hindered production and frustrated people, we began attacking root causes. Workarounds, long accepted as "just the way things are," were no longer tolerated. Teams were engaged directly to identify and eliminate barriers.

Throughout the journey, we made sure compensation reflected the market. Wages were raised multiple times, reinforcing that Spectrum valued its people and was willing to invest in them.

Equally important was the unwavering support from senior executives. They didn't just sign off on plans; they leaned in, removed barriers, and backed our efforts even when results weren't yet visible. That visible support told everyone: this time, things would be different.

The transformation didn't happen overnight, but the culture shifted. Employees who once felt trapped began to feel like they were part of something bigger. The plant's reputation improved both in the community and inside the company. What had been a place to avoid became a place where people wanted to contribute and grow. It ultimately became the flagship plant for the company and was recognized as the best manufacturing plant to work for in Montgomery County.

This Transformation Represents the Future

The Spectrum Brands turnaround demonstrates what becomes possible when manufacturing leaders embrace this new reality. This wasn't about lowering standards or accepting mediocrity—quite the opposite. By creating an environment of trust, transparency, and shared purpose, the plant achieved levels of performance that command-and-control approaches never could.

The transformation required every principle you'll learn in this book, working together as a system:

Data transparency replaced management secrecy, giving everyone visibility into real problems (Chapter 3).

Storytelling with numbers connected daily work to business outcomes that employees could understand and influence (Chapter 4).

Strategic prioritization focused energy on changes that mattered most instead of scattered firefighting (Chapter 5).

Business case thinking justified investments in people and systems with measurable returns (Chapter 6).

Empowered supervisors gave frontline leaders time and tools to lead their teams (Chapter 7).

Partnership across functions aligned HR, finance, and operations toward shared goals (Chapter 8).

Visible culture changes reinforced new expectations through consistent actions, not just words (Chapter 9).

Engagement isn't just an internal advantage—it's a customer advantage. When employees believe their work matters and take pride in how it's done, customers notice. They see it in the quality of the product, the reliability of delivery, and even in the tone of every interaction.

A disengaged workforce might still get the order out the door, but an engaged one delights customers and makes them want to come back. That's why building trust and purpose inside the plant is inseparable from building loyalty and growth outside of it.

The workforce challenges facing manufacturing aren't going away. If anything, they'll intensify as competition for talent increases and workforce expectations continue to evolve. The plants that thrive will be those led by people who understand that engagement drives performance, that transparency builds trust, and that respect is earned through action, not demanded through position.

This book will teach you how to become that kind of leader— one who can bridge the gap between business requirements and human motivation, creating environments where both performance and people flourish.

CHAPTER 2

A CULTURAL PULSE CHECK

The last chapter ended with a truth every site leader eventually learns—we need the employees much more than they need us. But before we can earn their trust or ask for their commitment, we must understand the environment they're working in. Culture shapes everything: what people believe, how they behave, and whether they choose to engage or just comply.

Leading from the middle starts with seeing clearly—and the first thing you have to see clearly is your culture.

Have you ever noticed that when you walk into someone else's manufacturing facility, certain things just jump out at you—things you're pretty sure the people who work there every day can't see?

Housekeeping is an obvious one, but it goes beyond that. You notice general working conditions—the lighting, the temperature, the level of dust control, and the state of break rooms, locker rooms, and restrooms. Those creature comforts send powerful signals about whether people take pride in their environment and whether leaders truly care about the well-being of their teams.

You also notice signs of commitment to safety, examples of 5S, and how people interact with each other. Within minutes, you start forming impressions about trust, discipline, and pride— or the lack of them.

What we need to learn to do is see those same things in our own facilities. The ability to look at your plant with an outsider's eyes—to step back, notice what's visible, and interpret what it says about how people think and feel—is one of the most important leadership disciplines there is.

Here's something we've learned after visiting countless plants: you can read the culture of a facility in minutes.

Why This Matters Before You Start

Before you try to adopt the principles in this book, you need to understand your starting point. Culture either accelerates or undermines every technical solution you'll implement.

Strong data systems won't help if people don't trust the numbers. Clear priorities won't stick if everything is treated as urgent. Partnerships won't form if functions are protecting their turf. Supervisors can't lead if they're buried in firefighting mode.

Culture isn't abstract—it's the foundation that determines whether your improvement efforts take root or get rejected like a bad transplant.

I learned this the hard way. Early in my career, I stepped into a leadership role where the culture was so toxic it destroyed every attempt at progress. It became one of the most formative lessons of my life.

A Horror Story from the Top Floor

In the early 2000s, I accepted a COO role at an unnamed company. The CEO had seen what we accomplished at the Roanoke book plant and said, "Hey, come here and do that for us." It wasn't an easy decision after 23 years, but I made the move.

I had arrived at "the top floor" with a mandate and thought I could change the world. Instead, I walked into an organization that ignored—or flat-out violated—every principle in this book. On the shop floor, many employees felt demoralized. Among site leaders, fear ruled the day. And in the C-suite, decisions were driven by brute force and intimidation, not strategy or trust.

Have you ever heard the saying, "The beatings will continue until morale improves"? That was the environment.

The company paid its managers at the very top of the market range. That pay wasn't a reward for excellence—it was a necessity to keep people from leaving. It created the sense of being trapped. Many thought, where else can I go and make this money?

Bottom line: I failed to drive change or deliver results. In hindsight, a cultural pulse check might have warned me about what I was stepping into.

After just 18 months, I left—without another job lined up.

The lesson: These principles aren't optional. Ignore them, and the culture will eat you alive. Live them, and you give people a chance to win.

Culture Eats Strategy

There's a saying: culture eats strategy for lunch. That story is living proof. I walked in with a mandate and a strategy, but the culture devoured it before it ever had a chance.

The experience was painful and caused me to doubt myself. Yet it also gave me perspective I couldn't have gained any other way—a deeper understanding of how leadership really works, and how essential culture is to everything that follows.

That's why it's worth pausing before you start—to take an honest cultural pulse check.

A Simple Assessment

Take a walk through your facility with these questions in mind. Don't overthink them—just observe what you see, hear, and feel:

Relationships and Connection: Do people make eye contact when you walk by, or do they look away? Do leaders greet employees by name? Is there natural conversation and camaraderie, or does your presence create awkward silence? When teams interact, do you see mutual respect and collaboration?

Safety & Housekeeping: Is there an obvious, consistent commitment to safety? Are hazards clearly addressed and protective measures in place—or do employees work around unsafe conditions? Are work areas clean, organized, and well lit? Housekeeping isn't cosmetic—it signals whether leaders and teams take pride in the workplace and whether people believe their well-being truly matters.

Obvious Evidence of Workarounds: Look for the signs—cardboard acting as a shim or stabilizer, duct tape holding things together, handwritten notes taped to machines with warnings or instructions. These workarounds aren't just maintenance issues; they're cultural indicators. Do teams dig for root causes and fix things properly, or do they patch problems and move on? In healthy cultures, workarounds become the known villain—something to identify and eliminate, not accept and normalize.

Trust and Transparency: Do people speak openly about problems, or do they tell you what you want to hear? When you ask, "How's it going?" do you get real answers or generic responses?

Information Flow: Is data visible, current, and meaningful to the people doing the work? Or is information hoarded, outdated, or irrelevant to daily decisions?

Leadership Presence: Do leaders spend time where the work happens, or are they mostly in offices and conference rooms? When they're on the floor, are they listening and learning, or inspecting and correcting?

Cross-Functional Dynamics: Do different areas work together toward shared goals, or do they operate in silos with competing priorities?

Getting an Outside Perspective

If you've been in your role for more than a year, you've probably adapted to your environment. What feels normal to you might look dysfunctional to fresh eyes.

Consider inviting someone you trust—a peer from another facility, a mentor, or an outside consultant—to walk your plant with you. Reach out to us if you think we can help. Ask them to be brutally honest about what they see. Their observations might reveal blind spots that have faded into your background.

Every chapter ends with a Cultural Pulse Check—a chance to pause and ask, "How does this show up in my plant?" These quick reflections help you measure progress, spot new blind spots, and guide conversations with your team.

Remember: you can't change what you can't see clearly. Take the pulse first, then prescribe the medicine.

Closing: From Culture to Clarity

Culture is what people see, feel, and live every day. It's visible in how they work, how they solve problems, and how they respond when no one's watching. But as a leader, your job isn't just to notice it—it's to understand it, shape it, and align it with purpose.

Once you've learned to see your culture clearly, you're ready for the next step: learning to see your data clearly. Because just like culture, data tells a story—if you know how to look for it.

PART II

DELIVERING RESULTS

INTRODUCTION

"FEVERISHLY FIGHTING TO EXCEED OUR KPIS EVERY HOUR OF EVERY DAY..."

That line—borrowed from a friend and colleague's email signature—captures the heartbeat of a site leader's job. Part II of this book is about that job in its simplest form: finding problems, fixing them, and delivering results.

Bottom line: your role is to make things run better tomorrow than they did today.

But we all know, not all "improvements" are created equal. Some create lasting gains that compound over time. Others feel good in the moment but fade quickly. And some aren't improvements at all, just favorable circumstances that make things look better than they really are.

Over time, we've found it helpful to think about improvement in five levels.

The sequence starts at Level 0 because the first "level" isn't improvement, it's the illusion of it.

Level 0: The Mirage

Sometimes what looks like progress is just a coincidence of good conditions—a week with fewer changeovers, an easy product mix, or a lull in quality issues. When conditions return to normal, the "improvement" disappears.

That's why we begin at zero: no real change has occurred.

Example:

A packaging line shows a sudden bump in output. The data reveals the real story: they happened to run fewer product variations that week, eliminating most changeover time. Nothing structural improved about the line's capability; performance only looked better because the variables shifted.

Takeaway:

Before celebrating performance gains, understand why they happened. If you can't trace improvement to a specific change you made, you may be looking at a mirage, not progress.

Level 1: Just Work Harder

Sometimes the "improvement" comes from pure effort. People dig deeper and push harder, like a team heading into a demanding season or preparing for a critical customer deadline. A leader gives a pep talk, rallies the team, and everyone leans in. Through extra focus, longer hours, and sheer determination, performance rises.

That's discretionary effort and it works…for a while. But it's not sustainable. Energy fades, fatigue sets in, and the gains disappear once the pressure lifts.

Example:

Heading into a peak production season, you challenge the team to finish strong. Crews put in extra hours, supervisors stay late, and for a few weeks output climbs. It's an impressive response to the challenge, but nothing about the process or the system changed. When the rush ends, so does the improvement.

Takeaway:

Celebrate and reward the effort—it shows commitment and pride. But recognize it for what it is: a temporary lift, not a lasting gain. True improvement begins when the system performs better without extraordinary effort.

Level 2: The Hawthorne Effect

Sometimes improvement happens simply because people know they're being observed or measured. A new metric, dashboard, or management initiative shines a spotlight on performance, and attention alone sparks better results. Visibility creates energy, conversations increase, and everyone leans in just a little more.

The improvement is real, but it's surface-level. Once the novelty fades or leadership attention shifts elsewhere, the extra energy fades too. Nothing in the process or habits has changed yet.

Example:

A site installs new real-time production displays. For the first few weeks, operators watch the numbers closely, react faster to downtime, and output jumps noticeably. But over time, the display becomes part of the background noise, and performance returns to its prior level.

Takeaway:

Visibility inspires focus but focus without follow-through doesn't last. Use that surge of attention to uncover deeper issues and build habits around the data. The goal isn't just to see more—it's to act differently because of what you see.

Level 3: The Sustainable Hawthorne

This is where improvement becomes more than a short-term reaction—it starts to take root in people's daily routines. The gains are real because they come from changed behavior: greater attention, faster response, and stronger ownership.

But this improvement still depends on human effort. It remains "sustainable" only as long as the team keeps its focus and energy high. It's vulnerable to shifting priorities, personnel changes, or simple fatigue. Nothing in the process has fundamentally changed yet the improvement lives in people's habits and discipline.

Example:

A department begins daily production huddles with visible scoreboards for uptime and scrap. Supervisors coach on the floor, operators track progress, and results improve week after week. But when a new initiative diverts attention or a key leader moves on, meetings get shorter, updates less frequent, and momentum slips.

Takeaway:

Behavioral improvements are powered by human focus. Protect them by reinforcing routines, recognizing effort, and keeping attention where it counts. When discipline becomes habit, the "Sustainable Hawthorne" stage can last, but it won't sustain itself.

Level 4: Structural Change

This is where lasting ROI lives. The process itself changes— equipment is redesigned, constraints are removed, or systems are improved so that success no longer relies on extra attention or heroic effort. Once structural change occurs, performance stabilizes. It's built into how the work happens; not how hard people work.

Example:

A chronic jam point on a conveyor causes repeated micro-stops. Instead of posting an operator to clear jams faster, engineering redesigns the transfer mechanism. The jams disappear permanently, freeing both capacity and attention for better work.

Takeaway:

Fix the system, not just the symptom. Structural change eliminates the root cause and sustains performance without constant supervision. It creates confidence, stability, and a foundation for continuous improvement that compounds over time.

The Path Forward

Execution isn't about chasing every metric or working harder every day. It's about recognizing what kind of improvement you're achieving—and leading your team toward the changes that last.

Mirages teach you to dig deeper into data.

Discretionary effort shows you what's possible when people care.

The Hawthorne Effect proves that visibility matters.

The Sustainable Hawthorne demonstrates the power—and the limits—of focus and behavior.

And Structural Change is where lasting capability lives.

Each chapter that follows gives you tools for climbing these levels—seeing clearly, finding the right problems, focusing energy where it matters, building partnerships that multiply your impact, and creating a culture that sustains progress.

And that journey starts with clarity. Before you can improve anything, you must see it.

The next chapter begins where every lasting improvement begins — with data. Because until you can measure what's real, you're leading by instinct, not insight.

CHAPTER 3

DATA—THE FOUNDATION FOR EVERYTHING

Quick Self-Check: What Kind of Leader Are You?

Before we talk about how data drives performance, take a quick look at how you use it.

Over time, we've found that most leaders fall somewhere on a simple 2×2 matrix defined by two dimensions:

- **Awareness** – how much you understand the power of data.
- **Engagement** – how willing you are to use it.

When you plot those two, four distinct leadership types emerge.

The Builder (High Awareness / High Engagement)

Builders use data as a bridge between people and performance. They don't chase numbers, they use them to tell stories, create alignment, and build trust.

Visibility isn't about control; it's about empowerment. In their plants, data belongs to everyone. Builders make performance visible and meaningful so every person can connect their work to results.

The Veteran	The Builder
High Awareness Low Engagement	High Awareness High Engagement
The Hero	The Fighter
Low Awareness Low Engagement	Low Awareness High Engagement

Their operations run with clarity and purpose because data has become a shared language—a conversation, not a report.

Keep building: Focus on clarity, not complexity. Use data to drive dialogue, not dictate outcomes. The more your people understand what the numbers mean, the faster your culture—and your performance—will improve.

The Fighter (Low Awareness / High Engagement)

If this is you, you're not alone—it's the most common. Fighters live in crisis-management mode, juggling problems day after day. You're working hard to improve performance, but every day feels like drinking from a fire hose.

Sometimes you're flying blind because reliable data doesn't exist. Other times, data exists but feels disconnected or overwhelming. Either way, you're reacting instead of leading—managing crises instead of preventing them.

The path forward: The principles in this book will help you move from firefighting to clarity and control, one disciplined step at a time.

The Veteran (High Awareness / Low Engagement)

These leaders understand the virtues of data but believe they already know what's happening. They walk the floor, talk to people, and trust their instincts. Data feels bureaucratic—something that slows decisions rather than sharpens them.

They often use data to confirm what they already know: "That person's our best operator." "That's our biggest problem." But when data is only used to validate opinions, it loses its power.

Experience is valuable, but it's not enough. Your walk-through shows a snapshot, not the full picture. Data doesn't replace intuition, it refines it.

Move forward: Pair your experience with evidence. Let data confirm or challenge what you think you know. When instinct and information align, decisions get faster and better.

The Hero (Low Awareness / Low Engagement)

Heroes thrive on urgency because they believe their value lies in the energy and expertise they bring to the table. They're constantly in motion, fixing problems, and saving the day. It feels productive and it earns praise.

Heroes often resist data because it replaces adrenaline with structure. It creates accountability by showing reality as it is. Data demands discipline, transparency, and follow-through. It's a different skill set.

They're not bad leaders; on the contrary, they tend to be the glue that holds the team together. They're just leading without a critical piece of the puzzle.

Move forward: Enhance your heroics with systems, and you'll become a force of nature.

Where Are You Now?

Take a moment to mark where you are, not where you hope to be.

Wherever you landed, the good news is this: data is the path forward.

The rest of this chapter shows how to use it to build clarity, connection, and control.

Everything Begins with Data

Throughout this book, one underlying assumption remains constant: everything begins with data.

Without it, the strategies, tools, and tactics discussed here are simply theories with no grounding in reality. You cannot effectively stand in the middle, and you cannot drive meaningful change, without having the right data at your fingertips.

The site leader's language is data. It's the fundamental currency of leadership. When you use clear, actionable metrics, you transform raw information into a story—a story that connects day-to-day operations with business objectives and gives context to every decision.

A data-driven approach ensures decisions aren't made in isolation. They're anchored in operational reality, creating a common language that resonates with both the top floor and the shop floor.

Whether you're identifying bottlenecks, tracking performance, or aligning daily activities with strategic objectives, data is the key to knowing where you are, where you're headed, and when to adjust course.

Without it, you're relying on intuition or incomplete information, and that's a blueprint for failure.

But let's be clear: data isn't a silver bullet. It's not a quick fix or a plug-and-play solution. Using it well requires effort, discipline, and often a new skill set. You must be willing to dig in, ask the right questions, and turn raw numbers into insight that drives action.

The leaders who do this well don't just collect data; they translate it into meaning. They use it to make expectations visible, connect performance to purpose, and lead with clarity instead of assumption.

The Starting Point: Creating Line of Sight

One of the most important ways to translate strategy into execution is by creating line of sight—helping the shop floor understand how their daily work impacts the business.

You have line of sight when you:

- Understand the parts of the business your role directly affects.
- Know the key metrics, how they're calculated, and how your actions influence them.

- Have a scorecard that clearly shows performance in real time.
- See how personal success fuels team success, and vice versa.
- Take ownership of your results and are accountable for them.

When employees can connect their daily actions to the company's success, ownership and engagement follow. They don't just complete tasks, they understand why those tasks matter.

When people know their contributions are measurable and tied to the business's bottom line, they start to care about outcomes, not just output. That shift—from activity to impact—is the foundation of a performance culture.

Once people understand how their work connects to results, the next step is to make that connection visible in real time.

The Power of Making It Visible

A common disconnect in manufacturing is the lack of real-time visibility.

That's where displays change the game.

Their real power isn't in the technology, it's in translation. They turn leadership expectations into something operators can see, own, and act on immediately.

When performance is visible:

- Operators get instant feedback and can correct problems before they escalate.
- Supervisors solve issues at the point of failure instead of explaining them tomorrow.
- Management can trust that information is current, accurate, and shared.

Displays speak the universal language of performance.

At their best, they don't just report, they spark conversation and collaboration.

Data becomes the translator, turning complex strategy into daily action that every person can understand and influence.

Motivation Through Visibility

At one site where we had just deployed our real-time displays, the impact showed up almost immediately. After the first day, the site leader sent a note celebrating a record-breaking run on one of their machines. His message captured the moment perfectly:

"Couldn't have done it without Flex."

He explained that the new displays gave the operator and crew a clear target to chase and visible feedback on their progress. The numbers weren't abstract; they were right in front of them.

That visibility changed everything. It gave the team ownership. They pushed harder, solved small issues before they became big ones, and hit a milestone they hadn't reached before.

That's the difference visibility makes. It turns performance from a management expectation into something the entire crew owns—moment by moment, run by run.

Still, that initial lift only matters if it lasts. As discussed in Part II, the goal isn't just to create a sustainable Hawthorne, it's to use that engagement to uncover and solve the problems behind the numbers. Displays should become more than a motivational trigger; they should evolve into a continuous-improvement tool, helping teams move from awareness to action, and from short-term excitement to lasting results.

Data Is Your Translator

Data connects two worlds that often speak different languages. It bridges corporate expectations and shop-floor reality.

When you ground conversations in clear, reliable metrics, you transform complexity into clarity. Strategy becomes something tangible—something that makes sense to the people doing the work.

Data allows you to lead in both directions at once:

- Upward, by giving executives confidence that actions align with business goals.

- Downward, by helping teams understand how their work impacts results.

That's the real power of data—it becomes the translator that keeps both groups aligned around the same truth.

Of course, data by itself doesn't fix anything. It only tells you that a problem exists. The real challenge for a site leader is to turn that raw information into a story people can understand, believe in, and act on.

Data creates visibility, but translation creates meaning. The best leaders use both: visibility to surface the truth, and translation to turn that truth into progress.

That's why the next step in this framework is so critical: finding the story in the data.

Pulse Check: Are You Grounded in Reality?

Ask yourself a few quick questions to test how well your operation is connected to reality:

Do you have real-time, accurate data, or are you relying on reports that are days old?

Are metrics visible, meaningful, and trusted by both leaders and teams?

Do your people have a common understanding of the goals and targets?

Can everyone—from operators to executives—describe what success looks like today?

If any of these answers make you hesitate, you've just identified your next improvement opportunity.

Closing Thought

Data brings visibility. It brings clarity. It brings confidence and decisiveness. It gives you solid ground to stand on.

But clarity alone isn't the finish line, it's the starting point. As a site leader, your job is to take what data reveals and turn it into understanding that others can act on.

Data connects the language of corporate expectations with the reality of shop-floor execution. It's the tool that lets you lead from the middle, translating strategy into daily action, and daily results into business outcomes.

You now have visibility, the hard facts that ground every conversation in reality.

But visibility alone doesn't move the needle. The next step is translation: turning numbers into meaning that drives action. In the next chapter, we'll learn how to find the story your data is trying to tell.

CHAPTER 4

FIND THE STORIES IN THE DATA: TRANSLATING DATA INTO DECISIONS

A t the end of the last chapter, we said it plainly:

Data creates visibility, but translation creates meaning.

Now it's time to turn that visibility into understanding—to uncover the story your data is trying to tell.

Data is one of the most powerful tools available to operations leaders. You cannot run a business effectively without it.

But here's the catch: data is useless—and maybe even dangerous—unless you know how to use it.

Data Without Translation Is Just Noise

It's not enough to collect information; you must turn it into a story that drives action.

Collecting data for its own sake only creates noise. The more numbers you dump into spreadsheets or dashboards, the harder it becomes for anyone to see what matters.

When leaders overload people with too much data, they don't get smarter, they get overwhelmed.

We've all seen it: a well-intentioned PowerPoint deck packed with charts and graphs that misses the point entirely. The data was there, but the story wasn't.

Data without translation is like a map without a legend—it may contain the truth, but no one can use it to get where they need to go.

Data only becomes powerful when it points people toward action. Without that translation, it just adds volume to the noise.

Find the Story in the Data

At Level 3 on the improvement ladder, visibility brings focus, but the next step is understanding. That happens when you find the story in the data.

Every data point represents something real—a job that ran well, a machine that struggled, a team that solved a problem, or one that hit a wall.

Your job as a leader is to find that story—to connect the numbers to what actually happened. When you do, people begin to understand not just what happened, but why.

The best stories are the ones that lead to action. They reveal patterns, expose friction, and point to what needs attention next. Without that context, even the best dashboards become wallpaper, numbers that fade into the background.

The Three-Part Story

Every meaningful data story has three parts:
1. What happened? – the visible result.
2. Why did it happen? – the context behind it.
3. What will we do next? – the action that moves the story forward.

When you teach your teams to ask these three questions, you turn data reviews into problem-solving sessions. They stop reporting and start learning.

Elephant Hunting: Spotting and Slaying the Hidden High-Impact Opportunities

On the shop floor, the primary goal can be summed up in a simple mantra:

"Get it in run. Keep it in run. At target speed."

That phrase captures the heartbeat of manufacturing. It's not about fancy strategy or abstract objectives; it's about keeping the machines running and meeting commitments.

The site leader's job is to find and fix the problems that get in the way, and that means using data to uncover the stories hiding in plain sight.

Across dozens of sites, three elephants appear almost everywhere.

Waiting – for materials, approvals, or quality checks.

One plant we worked with knew they had issues in a key department but couldn't quantify the impact. Once the data revealed how much time was lost to "waiting for materials," it gave them the proof they needed to justify a major process overhaul. The project wasn't cheap, but the ROI was undeniable.

Shift Transitions – the ramp-down and ramp-up during shift changes.

Shift transition losses are nearly universal, and most sites are shocked when they see the data. It's classic low-hanging fruit. Every plant should share one simple expectation: hand off a running machine. When one crew ramps down early and the next ramps up slowly, the chart tells the story, production dips appear like clockwork at every shift change.

Micro-Stops – frequent, short interruptions.

Micro-stops are the hidden beast. They rarely trigger alarms, but their cumulative impact can crush output and morale. At one site, a handful of recurring short stops on a critical asset were brushed off as "nuisances" until the data revealed their cost. Once the team fixed the root causes, run uptime doubled and scrap dropped sharply.

The lesson is simple: you don't really know which problems matter most until you can see their cost in hard numbers.

When used properly, data turns invisible friction into visible action.

Data Saves the Project (and Maybe My Job)

We had just invested in a custom-built machine to auto-mate the manufacturing of a niche product. The design was unique—developed with the OEM—and we had strict per-formance criteria for uptime, speed, and yield.

To say we had startup issues would be an understatement. The problem centered on two grippers designed to pick up a part and set it precisely into a frame. It wasn't working.

After weeks of frustration, a maintenance tech told me, "It's the parts; they're not consistent enough." He showed me how the plastic pieces were slightly warped.

That diagnosis spelled disaster: new materials, new molds, new supplier. It would have been a six-figure setback.

But we had data. I asked, "What does the system show for each gripper?" Sure enough, identical parts performed differently depending on which gripper handled them. That meant it wasn't the parts, it was the machine.

We shared our findings with the OEM, who quickly found a small design flaw and re-engineered replacements at no cost. The machine went on to meet its goals.

The moral: Without detailed, accurate data—the voice of the operator—we would have made a costly change that solved nothing.

Data Beyond the Plant Floor

Once you learn to find the story at the plant level, the same skills scale upward.

The patterns you uncover on the floor can reshape how your company thinks about pricing, product design, and profitability.

Data isn't just for solving operational problems, it can reshape business decisions at the highest level. The same insights that drive equipment and process improvements can also influence how you price products, set priorities, and hold partners accountable.

The Product That Was Breaking Us

We had a product with strong market share. On paper, it looked like a winner: steady volume, loyal customers, healthy margins. On the floor, it was a nightmare.

The components were beyond our equipment's capability. Operators dreaded running it. Quality inspectors flagged defects constantly. Maintenance was always chasing something. Everyone knew it was a problem, but no one could prove how bad it was.

Then we used data to quantify the impact.

We tracked the true cost—excessive downtime, elevated scrap rates, constant adjustments, and the toll on adjacent runs when changeovers took twice as long as they should. When we added it all up, this "good product" was a loser.

But data doesn't just expose problems, it creates conversations.

We brought the story to R&D and Marketing: "Here's what this product is costing us. Can we redesign the packaging to align with our equipment capabilities while still meeting customer needs?"

They engaged. Sourcing found better materials at the same cost. Sales supported the change because we showed them facts, not complaints. R&D developed packaging that our equipment could handle reliably.

The result became a case study: productivity increased to acceptable levels, quality improved, and absenteeism no longer spiked when that job appeared on the schedule.

The lesson: Data turned a manufacturing headache into a cross-functional solution.

Without the numbers, we would have kept suffering in silence or worse, blamed the operators, the equipment, or each other.

With the data, we turned an invisible problem into a visible opportunity the entire organization could rally around.

The Real Power of Data

The same insights that fix a gripper or reduce micro-stops can also tell you which products to redesign, which to reprice, and which partnerships need honest conversations.

Data can sharpen your pricing, guide your capital investments, and protect you from making decisions based on tradition instead of truth.

But only if you do the work to find the story.

A few examples of where data becomes a business tool:

Target Setting – grounding performance goals in actual capacity, not wishful thinking.

Pricing – using real cost and efficiency data to sharpen quotes and improve profitability.

Product Design & Value Engineering – using downtime or scrap data to highlight redesign opportunities.

Product Portfolio – deciding which products to grow, sustain, or exit.

Supplier Accountability – using facts to challenge quality, delivery, or cost issues.

Data becomes more than a plant tool it becomes a business tool. When used well, it aligns operations, strategy, and profitability.

Pulse Check: Are You Turning Data into Action?

Here's how you know if you're really using data well:

- Can your team explain a performance drop without opening a dashboard?
- When was the last time data changed your mind or started a conversation that led to real change?
- Do people ask for more data, or do they ask for better answers?

If your data reviews feel like storytelling sessions where people connect numbers to real problems and leave with clear next steps, you're doing it right.

If they feel like PowerPoint endurance tests where everyone nods politely and nothing changes, you're just collecting numbers.

Closing Thought

Data will tell you the truth, but the truth alone won't fix anything. Your job as a leader is to find the story in the data, share it in a way people can act on, and make the hard choice: what matters most right now?

The plants that win aren't the ones with the most data, they're the ones that know what their data is trying to tell them and have the discipline to act on it.

If you're not using data to drive action—to see clearly, decide confidently, and improve continuously—then what's the point?

Data tells powerful stories, but stories alone won't change outcomes. Every day, hundreds of those stories compete for your attention.

The next challenge for a leader is focus — deciding which ones to act on and which to leave alone.

That's where we go next: learning to separate motion from progress and mastering the discipline of doing less — better.

CHAPTER 5

WE CAN'T FIX EVERYTHING

For operations leaders, the challenge is balancing urgency with discipline—responding quickly without building a culture of reaction. The best leaders learn to separate motion from progress. They know that not every fix creates improvement, and not every improvement is worth the same effort.

The Two Pitfalls of Execution

The Quick Fix Trap - reacting fast and patching problems without ever addressing their real cause. It feels productive, but in the long run it builds a culture of workarounds.

The Prioritization Challenge - even when you know the root cause, you face more problems than resources. Choosing what to fix first isn't tactical; it's the difference between lasting progress and wasted effort.

Together, these two challenges define the early battleground for any leader. Solve them well and you create momentum. Fall into them and you'll spend your time chasing fires instead of building capability.

A Lesson in the Quick Fix Trap

We've all been there. The machine keeps jamming, so we tweak, swap, and adjust, hoping the next change sticks. It runs for a while, and everyone feels productive—like heroes—until the same problem returns on the next shift.

That's the danger of the quick fix: it feels good in the moment but rarely lasts. In fact, it often makes things worse because the root cause is still lurking, waiting to stop you again.

Activity Isn't the Same as Impact

In manufacturing, speed is survival. Leaders pride themselves on reaction time, putting out fires before they spread. But firefighting is deceptive:

Quick fixes feel productive but rarely solve the real problem. Short-term solutions often become permanent workarounds. Recurring issues frustrate teams, waste resources, and erode trust.

And here's where culture starts to slip. When you patch instead of fix, you're teaching your organization that "good enough" is acceptable. That cardboard shim, the duct tape on the guard, the handwritten note taped to a machine—all began as temporary solutions that someone decided were fine to live with.

Once you normalize patching over solving, the culture shifts from "fix it right" to "make it work somehow."

The progression is predictable:

- Problem occurs
- Quick fix is applied
- Problem returns
- Another quick fix is layered on
- Quick fix becomes permanent workaround
- Workaround becomes "just how we do things"

Before rushing into action, pause to understand the real source of the issue. Ask yourself: "Will this fix prevent the problem from happening again, or will it just help us react faster next time?"

And remember: the shop floor isn't a backdrop, it's the source. Go to the floor as a learner, not a tourist. Walk with curiosity. Look for disconnects between how work is supposed to happen and how it actually happens.

That's the essence of a Gemba walk.

Sidebar: A Quick Refresher on Gemba

Gemba is a Japanese term meaning "the real place." In Lean management, it refers to the actual location where value is created on the shop floor. A Gemba walk means observing the process firsthand, asking questions, and engaging with the team.

Key Principles:

- Go to the floor and witness work firsthand.
- Focus on processes, not individuals.
- Engage and communicate with the teams.
- Listen and learn.
- Show respect for everyone involved.
- Prioritize problem-solving and continuous improvement on site, where the work happens.

Takeaway: Don't confuse activity with impact. Quick fixes may buy time, but only root-cause solutions break the cycle that breeds workarounds.

The Prioritization Challenge: Focusing on What Matters Most

Even when you're solving real problems, another truth remains: there are always more issues than resources. You can't solve everything at once.

As one executive liked to say, "We can do anything, but we can't do everything." When you say yes to everything, you're really saying yes to nothing. Resources scatter, projects stall, and teams lose faith.

Some problems are loud but low impact. Others are quiet killers that erode performance. The leader's job is to tell the difference and focus the team on what truly matters.

When Chasing Everything Means Catching Nothing

At one plant, we fell into the trap without realizing it. Projects were everywhere—CI initiatives, capital upgrades, HR programs, training rollouts, quality improvements. If someone had a good idea, we added it to the list.

On paper, we looked ambitious. In reality, we were drowning.

The turning point came when people started asking, "What do you want me to work on first?" They weren't avoiding, they were overwhelmed.

There's an old saying: if a dog chases one rabbit, he'll catch it; if he chases two, he won't catch either.

We were chasing ten.

Projects dragged on for months. Teams worked hard but finished little. Effort was high, progress low, frustration growing. That's when we introduced a simple tool to bring order back to the chaos.

The Impact–Effort Matrix

We needed a straightforward way to separate noise from opportunity. The Impact–Effort Matrix helped us focus energy where it mattered most.

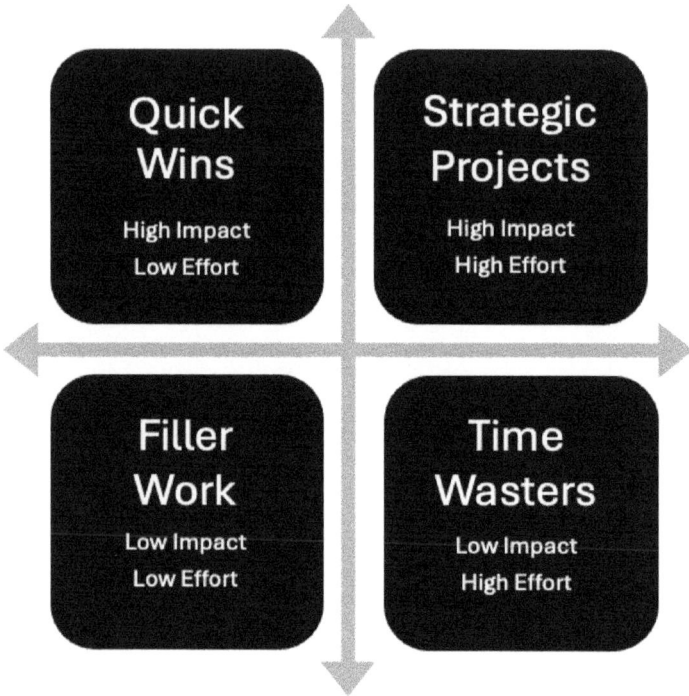

Quick Wins - High impact, low effort. Act on these immediately.

Strategic Projects - High impact, high effort. Invest wisely; these move the business.

Fillers - Low impact, low effort. Do them if time allows, but don't mistake them for progress.

Time Wasters - Low impact, high effort. Say no, defer, or kill these.

Real-Life Example: Plotting the Chaos

Priorities shift, markets move, customers change course, and what was urgent yesterday may not matter today.

To stay grounded, our leadership team met quarterly to evaluate every active project—CI initiatives, capital investments, HR programs, training efforts—using the matrix.

Each leader brought their list on sticky notes and posted them on the board. The outcome was both predictable and liberating.

Some "critical" initiatives turned out to be draining energy with little return. One "urgent" packaging change proved to be a costly customer preference, not a requirement so we killed it.

New Quick Win opportunities always surfaced. Often, newly discovered elephants exposed projects that gave us immediate traction with minimal effort.

Strategic projects got a fresh look. If the business case still held, we doubled down. If conditions had shifted, we deferred or re-scoped rather than throwing good money after bad.

The shift was dramatic. People stopped asking what to prioritize because they could see it. Teams finished projects instead of starting new ones. Energy returned because effort was finally translating into results.

The quarterly discipline gave us permission to say no to yesterday's priorities and focus on what mattered today. Without that reset, we would have stayed busy instead of effective.

We stopped chasing multiple rabbits. We picked one, caught it, and moved to the next.

Bringing It Together

Two Rules for Real Progress:

Avoid Quick Fixes: Solve problems the right way.

Prioritize What Matters: Solve the right problems.

As an operations leader, your job is to find legitimate problems and fix them. That means resisting the lure of band-aids and having the courage to say no to low-value work.

Bottom Line

Doing the right things, the right way, is how leaders escape the cycle of firefighting.

Prioritization ensures you're investing effort where it matters. Root-cause thinking ensures the solutions stick.

Pulse Check:
Are You Creating Impact or Just Activity?

- Do the same problems keep coming back despite repeated "fixes"?
- Are quick fixes becoming permanent workarounds?
- Are people constantly asking you to help them prioritize? (That's a red flag.)
- Is your team spread thin across too many initiatives, or focused on the few that move the needle?
- Do you regularly revisit priorities to ensure effort still matches business impact?
- Do you have a clear, shared process—like the Impact-Effort Matrix—to decide what gets attention and what doesn't?

Once you've focused the team on what truly matters, the next step is proving why it matters.

To win resources and support, you must connect operational pain to business impact.

In the next chapter, we'll translate improvement into the language every executive understands — return on investment.

CHAPTER 6

SPEAKING THE LANGUAGE OF ROI

Data tells you where to look. ROI tells you where to act.

Every operation has a list of known problems—machines that underperform, setups that take too long, quality issues that never quite go away. Spotting them isn't hard; every site leader can do that. The real test is turning those problems into investments that get funded and fixed.

When you can translate operational friction into business impact, you stop being a cost center that consumes resources and start becoming a profit center that generates them. You move from asking for money to presenting opportunities for return.

In earlier chapters, we focused on visibility and understanding—how to capture reliable data and uncover the stories it tells. Now comes the next step: using those stories to make a business case that compels action. This is where operational insight becomes influence and where data turns into decisions.

From Elephants to Investment Opportunities

Remember the elephants from Chapter 4—waiting for materials, shift-transition losses, and micro-stops that quietly eat away at throughput. Each one of those elephants is more than an operational nuisance; it's a business case waiting to be made.

That recurring micro-stop that "nobody could measure"? Now you can show it's costing $100 K annually in lost capacity. That's not a maintenance issue; it's an ROI case ready to be written.

This is the power of speaking the language of ROI. When you connect the cost of inefficiency to the return of improvement, the conversation changes. What once sounded like a complaint from operations now sounds like an investment opportunity for leadership.

When Survival Depends on ROI: A Plant on the Brink

"Are you here to shut us down?"

That was the first question an employee asked when I introduced myself as the new VP of the plant. I had just moved my family to take the job. The facility was a marvel—automated, beautifully designed, and staffed for 24/7 production.

And it was losing money.

The market had shifted. Our product mix was too narrow, our costs too high, and our volumes too low. Six months later, corporate confirmed what everyone feared:

"We're evaluating whether to move your work to a larger facility. The overhead here can't be supported by current demand."

The message was clear: either fix it fast or face closure.

I pulled the leadership team together with a simple statement: "Not on our watch."

This wasn't the time for incremental improvement. We needed a complete overhaul of the business model, something bold enough to change our economics and our future.

We Used Data to Define the Problem Precisely

The issue wasn't just "low volume." It was structural. Offshore competitors were producing similar work at prices we couldn't match.

We used data to pinpoint the impact:

- Our headcount was built for high-volume production we no longer had.
- Labor cost per unit was inflated by excess capacity.

- Overstaffing allowed inefficiencies to hide—there was always enough slack to work around problems instead of fixing them.

The math was brutal: our cost per unit made us uncompetitive. We had to redefine what we produced, for whom, and why.

We Calculated the Financial Impact of a Fundamental Solution

We couldn't win on price. But we could win on speed. Offshore suppliers required long lead times and large minimum orders. We could fill the gap they created—fast turnaround, short-run flexibility, and just-in-time responsiveness.

That meant:

- Expanding our capabilities beyond the plant's original narrow focus.
- Partnering with sales to redefine the market we served.
- Reducing headcount to match new demand levels—a painful but necessary reset.

Using continuous improvement not just to optimize what we had, but to build entirely new capabilities.

We set aggressive targets for cycle time, productivity, and quality. The workforce rallied. They knew what was at stake.

The Transformation

The company didn't close the plant—quite the opposite.

Sales redirected their efforts. The market responded. The plant delivered.

Volume grew. Profitability soared.

Many of the employees we had to release eventually returned, proud to be part of the turnaround they once thought impossible.

And the transformation went beyond the numbers. The same plant that had once feared for its future later earned **VPP Star Certification**, the highest OSHA recognition for safety and employee involvement. It became the first manufacturing facility in Virginia to earn that distinction.

That recognition wasn't just about safety; it was proof of a cultural shift. What began as a financial turnaround became a complete transformation in how people thought, worked, and led.

The Lesson

This wasn't just an operational fix; it was a full-scale business reinvention. ROI thinking scaled from machine-level repairs to market-level strategy.

When you can demonstrate clear, measurable impact—when you can show leadership that bold change makes business sense—you earn the confidence and the resources to transform more than equipment. You transform the business itself.

(An expanded version of this story appears in the Fortune magazine case study at the end of this book.)

Getting Capital Projects Approved

From Operational Insight to Executive Buy-In

Turning good ideas into funded projects isn't about finding the right form, it's about speaking the right language. Most companies already have standardized CapEx templates and approval processes. Your advantage comes from how well you use them to tell a story that makes business sense.

The goal isn't to reinvent the process. It's to make your data so clear, your logic so sound, and your payback so compelling that approving your project becomes the obvious choice.

Define the Problem Precisely

Start where all credibility begins, with the facts. Avoid vague descriptions like "equipment reliability issues." Use the data you've already gathered through your elephant hunting:

- Downtime frequency and duration
- Scrap and rework rates
- Overtime hours tied to breakdowns or slow setups
- Crew size requirements versus benchmark targets
- Changeover-time variation or quality fallout

When you describe problems this way, executives who have never set foot on the floor can still see what's happening. Data makes your problem real.

Quantify the Full Cost of the Problem

This is where most proposals fall short. The direct cost of downtime or scrap is easy to estimate, but the indirect costs are often what kill profitability.

- Lost production capacity = delayed shipments and missed revenue.
- Scrap = wasted material and rework hours.
- Overtime = higher labor cost plus hidden fatigue and turnover risk.
- Unreliable processes = damaged credibility with customers and internal stakeholders.

By showing the true cost of the problem, you elevate it from a maintenance concern to a business exposure.

Translate the Solution into Financial Terms

Once you've defined the cost, show the return. Estimate capacity gains, cost reductions, or risk mitigation using conservative assumptions. If the company requires a five-year payback model, build it on solid operational understanding, not wishful thinking.

If your plant's ROI threshold is 20%, find out what that really means in dollar terms. Partner with finance early. They'll help you translate throughput gains or downtime reductions into the P&L language executives expect.

Address Risk Honestly

CapEx templates almost always include risk sections—implementation challenges, timing conflicts, or potential alternatives. Be direct and balanced. Acknowledge the risk, describe the mitigation, and show that you've thought it through.

Credibility doesn't come from perfect plans; it comes from realistic ones.

Make It Easy to Say Yes

Capital committees are constantly juggling competing priorities. You improve your odds when you remove friction from their decision.

- Align your project with strategic priorities and budget cycles.
- Schedule implementation during planned downtime windows.
- Minimize operational disruption.

A good idea that fits cleanly into the business rhythm gets approved faster than a great idea that causes chaos.

Speak the Language of Business

Capital approval isn't an expense conversation; it's an investment competition. Executives are deciding where to place the next dollar for the greatest return. Understanding that dynamic changes the way you frame your proposal and how you respond to objections.

Common Objections and How to Respond:

"We don't have the budget this year."

Show payback in ROI terms. If your project returns its investment in less than 18 months, position it as an opportunity, not a cost. Budgets are tight, but strong returns always find funding.

"The payback period is too long."

Highlight the benefits the spreadsheet doesn't capture—safety improvements, quality gains, delivery reliability, customer retention. Quantify these where you can; they often turn "soft" benefits into hard savings.

"This isn't the right time."

Demonstrate the cost of waiting. Reliable data will show the curve—rising downtime, growing maintenance costs, declining performance. Often, the cost of inaction dwarfs the cost of action.

Bottom line: when you speak the language of ROI, "no" usually means "not yet." Stay consistent, keep refining, and keep bringing data that ties operational need to business value.

Building Your Track Record

This process works, not just once, but every time you apply it with discipline.

When I took responsibility for a plant full of obsolete equipment and decades of workarounds, modernization looked impossible. So, we started small. We documented every machine's speed, output, crew size, and maintenance cost. Each upgrade, from minor overhauls to major automation, was justified with a clear ROI case.

Over eight years, we submitted more than a hundred Capital Appropriation Requests (CARs). None were denied.

That track record wasn't luck. It was the result of three consistent disciplines:

We only proposed projects with real payback.

If a project couldn't meet the ROI threshold, we either refined it until it could or walked away. Saying "no" to ourselves built trust that our "yes" meant something.

We previewed borderline projects with leadership.

When a proposal was strategically important but financially tight, we never surprised anyone. We asked for early feedback and listened. It showed respect for their judgment and gave us insight into timing and readiness.

We treated every CAR like a business case.

Each request told a complete story: what was broken, what it cost us, how we'd fix it, and what the return would be. We didn't ask for money, we offered investment opportunities.

We started with small wins—a $25K overhaul with an 11-month payback, then a $150K automation project that paid off in 15 months. Every project delivered the results we promised.

As our track record grew, so did leadership's confidence. Soon our smaller CARs weren't scrutinized like everyone else's. By year five, we were getting approval for much larger transformations—not because of politics, but because we had proven we understood the business as well as the equipment.

We had a vision for transforming the plant and we proved it made business sense, one project at a time.

Pulse Check: Are You Speaking the Language of ROI?

- Do you frame operational problems with specific metrics instead of general complaints?
- Can you translate those metrics into clear financial impact for decision-makers?
- When facing objections, do you respond with data that shows the cost of waiting?
- Have you built a track record of delivering on the financial results you promised?
- Are you seen as someone who asks for money—or someone who creates investment opportunities?

Transition: From ROI Thinking to Execution Power

Turning problems into funded projects is only half the job. The real payoff happens when those investments deliver—consistently, safely, and at the level of excellence you promised. That part doesn't live in a spreadsheet. It lives on the shop floor.

Execution is where credibility is earned. It's driven every day by department managers and front-line supervisors who turn plans into performance. The people who make sure the new equipment runs as expected, the new process sticks, and the promised gains show up in the numbers.

These leaders translate investment into impact. They're the ones who take the abstract logic of ROI and make it real in uptime, quality, and throughput. When they execute well, they validate your business case and strengthen your influence across the organization.

But as the scope of your improvement efforts grows, so does your need for allies beyond the plant floor. Finance helps sharpen the numbers. Engineering helps scope solutions. Supply chain, quality, and HR remove obstacles that can derail even the best ideas.

The most effective site leaders build bridges—between execution and analysis, between shop floor and boardroom. They surround themselves with indispensable partners who can strengthen their cases, navigate corporate processes, and help turn good ideas into lasting results.

That's where we turn next.

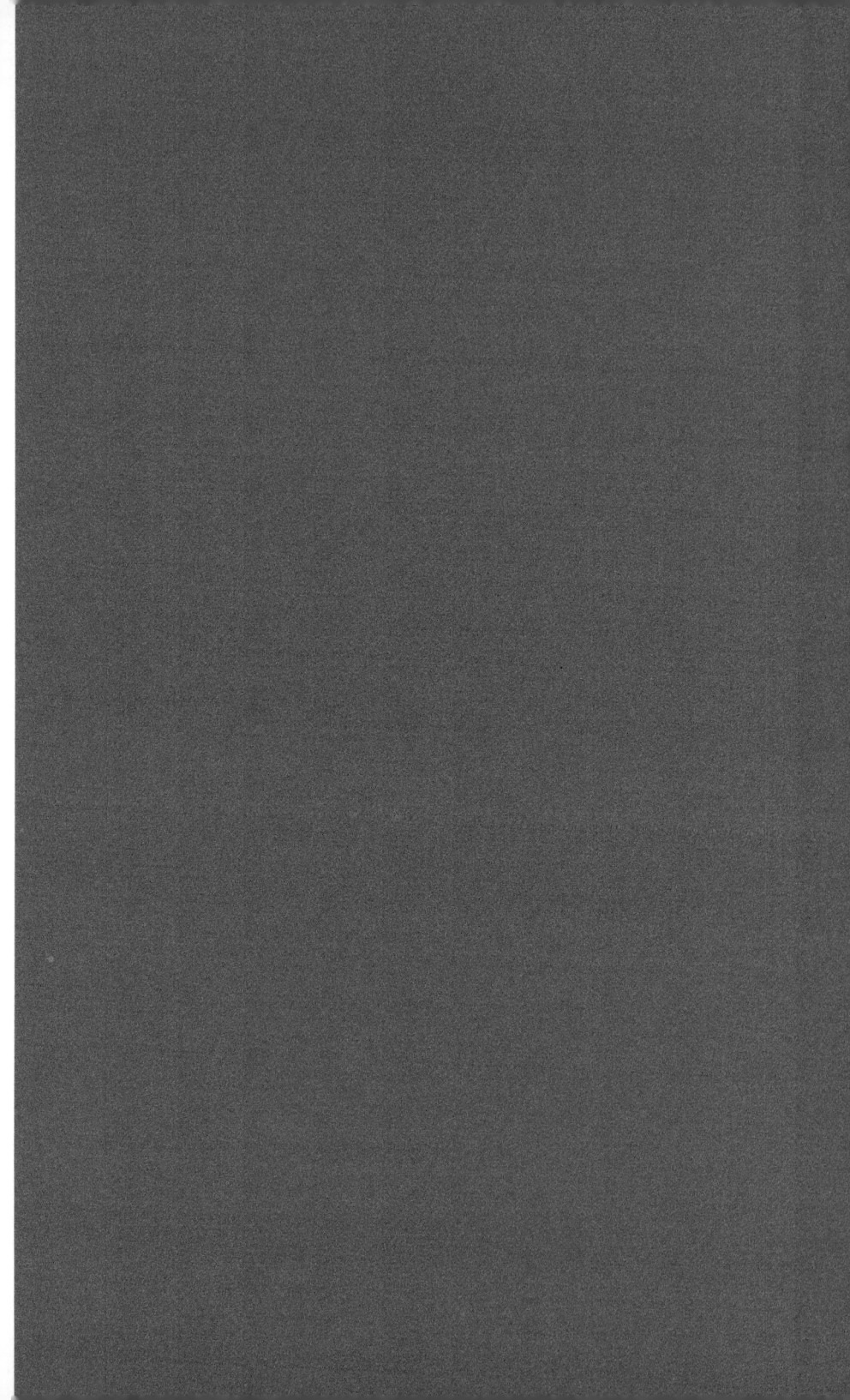

PART III:

LEADING THROUGH PEOPLE

From Numbers to People: Where Execution Lives.

Data creates visibility. Prioritization creates focus. ROI thinking builds credibility. But sustainable results come from leaders who make all of it stick.

Part III focuses on leadership—the supervisors who lead, the managers who align, the partners who multiply impact, and the culture that keeps it all running. These chapters translate the what of execution into the who that delivers it.

CHAPTER 7

LINE SUPERVISORS: ORGANIZATIONAL DUCT TAPE

Picture this: it's 6:30 a.m. and your day-shift supervisor is already on the floor, trying to get a packaging line back up that went down overnight. By 7:00, their phone is blowing up with questions from the warehouse about a missing pallet. At 7:15, they're crawling around with a flashlight helping maintenance find a hydraulic leak. By 8:00, they're two crises deep and didn't make it to the daily production meeting because now a customer complaint has landed on their desk.

Sound familiar?

Here's what most organizations miss: supervisors are the most important people in the building and the most overloaded. When you think a supervisor isn't cutting it, it's almost never because they're disengaged or untalented. It's usually the opposite—they're drowning in everything except actual supervision.

Supervisors Become the "Catch-All"

In most plants, supervisors are the default answer to one question: "Who's going to handle this?"

Equipment breaks? Call the supervisor.

Rush order needs babysitting? Supervisor.

HRs tied up and a new hire needs training? Supervisor again.

Quality issue pops up? The supervisor will "figure it out."

One at a time, those things don't seem like much. Stack them together and supervisors spend their days running around putting out fires instead of leading their teams.

Giving the Job Back to Supervisors

Draw boundaries be clear on what is and isn't a supervisory task. Find out what consumes their time and decide if that's what they should be doing. If not, eliminate it or reassign it.

Fix structural gaps: don't use supervisors as plug-and-play fillers for missing roles, such as quality or inventory management.

Cut meetings: if they don't need to be there, don't make them be there.

Automate the headaches: ditch or digitize repetitive reporting tasks (supervisor reports, manual reconciliations, end-of-shift summaries). Minimize their admin burden.

Protect floor time: let them be where it matters most, walking the floor, coaching, and solving problems with their teams.

Supervisors are not Swiss Army knives. They're the hinge between management's plans and daily reality. If that hinge gets jammed, the whole system creaks.

A Story from the Floor

When I took over one struggling site, the supervisors worked a "4×10" schedule—four ten-hour shifts. In theory, that left them three days off. In practice, Fridays (and some Saturdays) got added to catch up on production.

Supervisors were putting in 60-hour weeks, often more. Sadly, most of that extra time wasn't spent leading. It was paperwork. Spreadsheets. Reconciling materials. Reports they didn't have time to touch on shift. By Friday, they weren't recharged, they were cooked.

No surprise, they were burned out and frustrated.

So, we rewrote the playbook:

Start with leadership: give real training, not just "how to run production." Coaching, conflict management, and how to think like leaders.

Take work off their plates: we hired an inventory clerk to handle material reconciliations. In one move, supervisors gained hours back and our accuracy shot up.

Protect time off: we built coverage so they could unplug on weekends and come back fresh.

The change was obvious. Supervisors left on time, spent their days with their teams instead of buried in spreadsheets, and stepped into being leaders instead of firefighters. Morale went up. So did safety. So did productivity.

Pulse Check: Are Supervisors Leading or Just Drowning?

Are your supervisors mostly leading or mostly plugging holes?

Did you promote them because they were great operators, or did you train them to be leaders?

Do they work reasonable hours, or is burnout baked into the job?

Do they connect teams across shifts or just slap duct tape on the cracks?

Culture doesn't flow from memos or posters. It lives or dies with the presence of frontline leaders. And if your supervisors are drowning, your culture is too.

CHAPTER 8

DEPARTMENT MANAGERS: THE TOUGHEST JOB IN THE PLANT

Ask any site leader who has the toughest job in the plant, and most will tell you: the department manager. They live between two worlds—the front line and the front office—and the pressure from both sides is relentless.

Early in my career, I did a short stint in sales as an account manager for a large customer. We were having a recurring issue we just couldn't get our arms around. I was walking through the production facility with a senior executive, talking about the problem and how a particular department wasn't doing what they needed to do to resolve it. The executive stopped, looked at me, and said, "Sometimes you have to either change the leader or change the leader."

That line stuck with me. It was the moment I realized just how critical department managers are, and how often they are blamed when things go wrong. They're close enough to touch the problem but not always empowered or supported enough to fix it.

If supervisors are the most important but least equipped, department managers have the toughest job but are the least appreciated.

They live in the narrowest space of all, between the site leader and the supervisors. From above, they absorb expectations for output, quality, cost, and safety. From below, they absorb the daily realities of shortages, breakdowns, and human exhaustion.

They're close enough to the floor to feel the pressure when a line goes down, yet far enough removed to see how those problems ripple across the business. One minute they're walking the floor, sleeves rolled up; the next they're in a conference room explaining performance to leadership.

More than anyone else in the organization, department managers are the critical link in the execution of strategy. They make hundreds of tactical decisions—about people, priorities, and resources—that determine whether a strategy succeeds or stalls. Their choices about how to deploy resources, who to assign to critical jobs, and when to take risks or play it safe all have ripple effects across the plant.

I once worked with a manager who staffed a critical equipment start-up based on who was most willing, rather than who was best prepared. The volunteers were eager and well-intentioned, but they lacked the experience needed for a smooth launch. When the ramp-up fell short of expectations, we had to make painful course corrections. The lesson was clear: leadership decisions can't follow the path of least resistance, they must be intentional, informed, and aligned with both short-term performance and long-term success.

It's a constant balancing act—too deep in the weeds and they lose perspective; too far removed and they lose credibility. And if they're honest, it sometimes feels like they spend half their time in the HR leader's office, working through performance problems or coaching through behavioral issues.

And sometimes, we make it even harder for them.

Too many site leaders fall into the trap of micromanaging their department managers by stepping into their meetings, second-guessing their calls, or inserting themselves into issues that should be handled one level down.

The more you step in, the less they step up. Micromanagement doesn't build capability; it breeds dependency. If you can't let go of the details, you'll never build the bench strength your plant needs to grow.

To be effective, they need a firm grasp of the technical and operational demands of their own department—the processes, equipment, materials, and people that make it run.

But that's not enough anymore. They also need to understand how their area connects to the business. They must be able to explain performance in both operational and financial terms: how downtime affects delivery, how yield impacts margin, how overtime or scrap shows up in the P&L.

The best managers use data as their language. They know that numbers alone don't tell the story, they reveal where to look. They dig into the data to find meaning, to understand why something happened, and to translate that story in a way leadership can act on, and teams can rally around. They connect the dots between what the business measures and what the operators experience—turning numbers into understanding and understanding into action.

Many plants treat department managers as conduits for communication, messengers for whatever is coming down from the top. The best site leaders know better. Managers don't just pass information up or down; they interpret it, give it context, and help others see what it means. They turn direction into action, confusion into clarity, and goals into results. When they're engaged, things move. When they're not, it all slows down.

The best managers also understand that their job isn't just to win within their department, it's to help the entire plant succeed. Success in isolation isn't success at all. When one department struggles, everyone pays the price eventually.

Real teamwork shows up when managers think and act beyond their own boundaries. They resist the temptation to optimize their metrics at someone else's expense, and they don't celebrate local victories that create global pain. Instead, they work together to balance priorities, share resources, and solve problems across functions.

It's easy to chase higher output by pushing problems downstream, but that's not leadership. Leadership means making the hard calls, sometimes sacrificing short-term gains for the greater good. It's seeing yourself as part of something bigger, a system where the goal is collective performance, not individual recognition.

When department managers operate that way, collaboration replaces competition, alignment replaces ego, and the plant starts to move as one. That's when real transformation happens.

Finally, great managers don't just run today's process, they reimagine tomorrows. Their vantage point lets them spot inefficiencies, constraints, and new ideas that could change the plant's trajectory. Too often, managers fall into a cycle of chasing incremental gains—another percent of productivity here, a few fewer defects there. Those improvements matter, but they're not enough.

The real difference-makers bring forward big ideas—step changes that improve productivity, reduce waste, or elevate quality in meaningful ways. As a site leader, set that expectation early: continuous improvement is the baseline; transformative ideas are part of the job.

What It Looks Like When It Works

You may remember the Spectrum Brands turnaround story from Chapter 1. The plant was struggling on every front—morale, safety, quality, and reputation—and the change that followed became one of the most meaningful experiences of my career.

What truly drove the turnaround was the team of department managers who stepped up and owned the journey. Individually, they were all high performers. But as a team, they were exceptional. They had each other's backs, and mine. They challenged one another, shared information freely, and aligned around a common purpose. When one department stumbled, the others stepped in to help. When priorities shifted, they adjusted together.

Nowhere was the concept of camaraderie, mentioned earlier in the cultural pulse check, more evident than with this group. There was genuine teamwork, respect, and admiration within our management team, and that spirit became contagious throughout the entire site. Employees saw how we interacted with each other—with trust, honesty, and good humor—and they began to mirror it. The tone we set at the leadership level became the standard for how people worked together throughout the plant.

That management team became the cultural backbone of the plant. They modeled trust, accountability, and collaboration in ways that made those principles real, not theoretical. They didn't just execute my vision, they co-created it. That was the moment I understood what real alignment looks like, not compliance, but shared ownership.

Their unity gave the supervisors the confidence to lead, and their consistency gave employees a reason to believe that "this time, things really are different."

The plant's turnaround wasn't about a single leader's strategy, it was about a team of managers who led together, stood together, and built something that lasted.

Your supervisors execute. Your managers orchestrate.

When they're equipped, appreciated, and aligned, your entire operation moves in rhythm. When they're not, the organization falls out of sync, and no amount of effort can make up the difference.

Develop them. Coach them. Hold them accountable. But also lift them up.

They are the bridge between leadership and execution, and the strength of that bridge determines how far your plant can go.

Pulse Check: Are You Building Your Bench?

Do you spend as much time developing your department managers as you do directing them?

Do your managers understand how their department's performance connects to the P&L, not just the production schedule?

When you review data, do your managers focus on numbers or on the story those numbers tell?

Are your managers investing in their supervisors the same way you're investing in them?

If one of your department managers left tomorrow, could someone on their team step up with confidence and clarity?

Building your bench doesn't happen by accident. It happens when you treat development as part of the job, not an extra task. The more capable your managers become, the stronger your supervisors will be, and the more resilient your entire operation grows.

CHAPTER 9

INDISPENSABLE PARTNERS: MORE THAN JUST SUPPORT

No operation succeeds in isolation. Every department depends on others to plan, supply, maintain, and support production — yet many of those functions don't report to you.

The best site leaders understand that delivering results requires collaboration beyond the boundaries of their own organization.

This chapter is about those indispensable partners — the people and functions you rely on every day, even if they don't work directly for you.

- The Finance Partner
- The HR Leader
- The Matrix

These aren't "support" roles. They're critical leadership functions, and your success depends on them. When they're empowered, aligned, and trusted, the plant performs differently.

Finance: The Storyteller Behind the Numbers

Great operations leaders don't just manage output—they manage outcomes.

To manage outcomes, you need someone who can connect the dots between the floor and the business impact. That's the role of a great finance partner.

They don't just report numbers. They help you find the operational reality behind the financial result. They:

- Tell the story behind the metrics
- Quantify the cost of inefficiencies
- Frame capital requests in business terms
- Show how improvement initiatives affect variances and budget attainment.
- Forecast so you can act early

They turn rows and columns into information that leads to the required operational focus. They make the business case behind every problem and solution. Without that translation, good ideas get lost in the noise. With it, you get traction.

What a Great Finance Partner Looks Like

A great finance partner has a seat at your leadership table. They don't just send reports, they attend your meetings, engage in discussions, and help your team see the story behind the numbers.

In previous chapters, we talked about finding the stories in the data. The finance partner does the same thing with financial reports—finding the stories hidden in the numbers and translating them into actionable insights that operations leaders and frontline teams can use to drive improvement.

They teach the financials, translating accounting language into operational meaning. They help managers understand how downtime affects margin, how scrap hits the P&L, and how productivity drives contribution.

They connect financial variances to what's happening on the floor, identifying trends and surfacing where attention is needed. When a variance appears, they don't just point it out, they help trace it to its root cause.

They participate in problem-solving and troubleshooting right alongside your managers, closing the loop between what's happening in operations and how it shows up in the financials.

The best finance partners don't just measure performance, they make it visible, understandable, and actionable. They don't just report on the past; they help shape the future.

HR: The Confidant, the Compass, and the Cultural Mirror

HR is often referred to as the policy police or the compliance officer. And to be fair, that's part of the job, and an important one. A great HR leader ensures that the organization operates in ways that are fair, consistent, and compliant with both policy and law. That role deserves respect. They're not trying to slow you down; they're helping you stay within the guardrails that protect both people and the business.

But compliance is only one dimension of what great HR partners do. At their best, they're your mirror, your compass, and your ally. They:

- Keep a pulse on your people
- Speak the hard truths others won't
- Help turn values into behaviors
- Protect culture by calling out drift
- Guide you through tough decisions with clarity and empathy

They help you see your blind spots and lead with both backbone and heart. When HR is reduced to policies and paperwork, culture decays. When HR is trusted, aligned, and respected—when they have a seat at the table—they become a multiplier.

What a Great HR Partner Looks Like

Great HR partners have an ear to the floor. They don't just track operational issues, they listen for cultural issues, behavioral patterns, leadership gaps, and communication breakdowns. They pay attention to the questions people are asking and, just as importantly, which ones need attention.

They help you separate what we call the *background radiation*—the everyday frustrations and disappointments that come with any group of people—from the issues that truly require your awareness, involvement, and action.

They translate those insights into specific actions and behaviors for the leadership team—what needs to change, what needs to be reinforced, and what you, as the site leader, personally need to do differently.

And they help you do it the right way. They coach you through how to deliver the right message, in the right setting, to the right audience. They give you candid feedback on how effectively you're doing it. They open your blind spots and show you where your own temperament or tendencies may be getting in the way.

With the right kind of relationship, a great HR leader becomes more than a partner, they become a leadership coach for you and your team.

Just like finance finds the story in the numbers, HR finds the story in the people—what's motivating them, what's frustrating them, and what they need to perform at their best.

The best HR partners don't just enforce the rules, they elevate the standard. They help leaders see that culture isn't something you manage; it's something you model every day.

Managing the Matrix

In a matrixed organization, you rely on multiple functions that directly impact your ability to execute and yet, they don't report to you.

They have their own bosses, their own priorities, and their own scorecards. Still, their choices shape your ability to get it in run, keep it in run, at target speed.

Planning is tasked with forecast accuracy and inventory turns. Those goals are vital, yet strategies that protect them can disrupt product sequence and make it harder to stay in run.

Quality guards the customer and the brand. Standards are non-negotiable, but meeting them without collaboration can mean more downtime, slower speeds, or higher scrap.

Sourcing is rewarded for driving down material cost. Lower-cost materials can introduce runability issues that prevent the plant from keeping it in run.

Sales wins business and keeps customers happy, sometimes making commitments that stretch capacity or capability.

IT protects the organization from cyber threats and manages competing priorities across the business. Without early involvement and executive air cover, they can look like a barrier, especially for shop-floor data systems.

Marketing & R&D design new products customers want but designs that ignore manufacturability can create endless production issues.

It's in these moments that the familiar refrain shows up: "They just don't get it."

But they do get it. They're faithfully executing the job they've been asked to do. Planning protects turns and working capital. Quality guards the customer. Sourcing drives cost out. Sales pursues revenue. IT shields the company. Marketing and R&D innovate for the future.

The problem isn't that they "don't get it." The problem is that, in a matrix, the "it" is different for each function. Unless someone bridges those differences, the conflicts all show up in the same place: on the shop floor.

Leading Through Influence

John Maxwell said, "Leadership is influence, nothing more, nothing less." In a matrixed organization, authority is limited. Influence is not.

The site leader's role isn't to fight with other functions. It's to build a coalition across them—reframing problems in ways that reveal the shared interest. That's how cross-functional win-wins are created.

When the Matrix Works

Our elephant-hunting process uncovered several improvement opportunities that touched multiple functions. Excessive changeover time, reactive scheduling, material issues, and outdated quality standards were all making it harder for the plant to stay in run.

We quantified the cost of excessive changeover time driven by reactive scheduling and worked with Planning to adjust sequencing, allowing us to reduce complex changeovers and create real capacity.

We created a cross-functional task force with quality, marketing, and sales. Reviewing product standards, we found many were unnecessarily tight. Together, we streamlined specifications aligned with equipment capability.

We partnered with sourcing to define material specs that fit our equipment. Rather than chasing the lowest price, they went to market with those specs and found suppliers who delivered both runability and competitive cost.

Marketing and R&D invited us in early on a new design. We selected materials that met customer attributes and ran reliably at speed, hitting innovation and manufacturability.

For data, we pulled IT in early to expand the shop-floor system. We explained the business case, secured leadership support, and treated them as a partner, not a service desk. They bought in and accelerated the project.

None of this happened because we controlled those functions. It happened because we built trust, used data to frame problems, and created win-wins across the matrix. Each partnership made it easier for the plant to do what matters most: get it in run, keep it in run, at target speed.

Matrix Pulse Check

Do functions operate in silos, guarding their own turf?

Are KPIs aligned across areas, or are they in open conflict?

Do incentive targets pull people together or drive them apart?

When priorities collide, is there a spirit of win-win, or win-lose?

Finance, HR, and matrix functions aren't obstacles to navigate around. They're allies to build with.

CHAPTER 10

CULTURE YOU CAN SEE

This chapter feels different—because it is.

The first nine chapters gave you tools, frameworks, and systems. This one is about something harder to measure but impossible to ignore: the daily behaviors that make all of it stick...or cause it to fall apart.

What leaders choose to notice, tolerate, and repeat becomes culture. Consider this a survey of the few behaviors that move everything else.

We're passionate about leadership. How leaders show up matters, not just for big decisions or crisis moments, but in every interaction, every walk through the plant, every conversation.

We made it a point to show up with energy, enthusiasm, and optimism. It was impossible to succeed every day (we're all human), but the effort mattered.

One day I learned how much it mattered when I discovered that the receptionist at one plant would give people a heads-up if I wasn't my usual self. My presence, good or bad, rippled through the organization.

That's the reality of leadership: you're never just managing operations or solving problems. You're setting the emotional and cultural tone for hundreds of people who are watching, interpreting, and responding to your every move.

This chapter is about real leadership, not titles, not org charts, but the leadership that shapes culture through presence, consistency, and follow-through.

What They're Watching For

That awareness of being watched isn't paranoia, it's leadership reality. One day, as I was walking the floor, I stopped to talk with an operator. He was widely respected, outspoken, and good at his job—someone I call an opinion leader.

He looked me straight in the eye and said:

"You know we're watching everything you do, right?"

It stopped me cold. He wasn't joking; he was speaking for the floor. They weren't just responding to my daily energy levels. They were watching what I prioritized, what I let slide, what I reinforced under pressure.

It's a universal truth of leadership: your people are constantly evaluating what you value based on your actions, not your words. They're looking for patterns that tell them what truly matters around here.

Culture Is What People See, Not What You Say

You can hang posters, share goals, and talk about values all day, but if your behavior doesn't match, the message falls flat.

Culture is defined daily in:

- What gets attention
- What gets ignored
- How leaders respond under pressure
- What's tolerated and what isn't

Beyond individual actions, people are watching for consistency. Do they know what they're going to get when they interact with you? Can they predict how you'll respond to problems, conflicts, or pressure? Do they see a constant connection between your words and deeds?

Consistency flows from authenticity.

Authentic leaders are consistent because they're genuinely themselves in every interaction. They don't perform different roles for different audiences. When you ground your decisions in operational truth—the data from earlier chapters—rather than what you think people want to hear, your responses become predictable and trustworthy.

Consistency isn't about being perfect it's about being true to your principles. When employees know you'll always ask for data before making decisions, they come prepared with facts. When they know you'll always prioritize safety over production, they don't hesitate to stop lines for safety concerns. When they know you'll follow through on commitments, they trust your promises.

The opposite—inconsistent leadership—is cultural poison. Leaders who are supportive one day and critical the next create anxiety. Leaders who preach safety but reward output above all else confuse priorities. Leaders who promise follow-up but forget create cynicism. When leaders react emotionally— especially in anger or frustration—they don't motivate; they intimidate. People stop taking initiative and start playing it safe. Over time, those inconsistencies chip away at credibility—the quiet erosion of integrity that's hardest to repair.

If you want to know what someone values, don't listen to what they say. Watch what they do consistently, especially under pressure.

Workarounds: Where Words and Actions Collide

Nowhere is the gap between what leaders say and what they tolerate more visible than in workarounds. They tell a story about what is accepted and tolerated, if not encouraged. They speak directly to inconsistency, what you do versus what you say.

Workarounds inflict pain on multiple levels. They create safety risks when people bypass proper procedures or use makeshift solutions. They compromise quality when "good enough"

becomes the standard. They kill productivity through ineffi-
cient processes everyone knows are broken but no one fixes.
The cultural damage is just the beginning, the operational
costs compound daily.

Workarounds are a nuisance, and they're everywhere: cardboard acting as shims, duct tape holding equipment together,
handwritten signs taped to machines with warnings and
instructions. Each one represents a problem someone decided
was acceptable to live with rather than fix.

It's hard work to eliminate them, but you will struggle to make
meaningful improvements if you don't. Workarounds send
a message about your actual standards, regardless of what
your policies say.

When workarounds are tolerated, the message is clear:
problems don't get solved here. That belief erodes trust, dis-
courages ownership, and normalizes cutting corners. Over
time, the culture shifts from solving to surviving.

When leaders spot workarounds, ask why they exist, and fix
the root cause, the signal flips. The culture says: problems
matter, people's voices are heard, and leadership follows
through. That's how trust grows and how performance follows.

The Workaround Walkaround

One leadership practice I came to rely on was the workaround
walkaround—walking the floor with the specific goal of spotting these patches.

At one plant, we found coat hangers propping hoses, cardboard patching machines, wooden shims stabilizing rails, and zip ties holding parts together.

We didn't demand immediate removal. As G.K. Chesterton said, "Don't ever take a fence down until you know why it was put up."

Each workaround was documented, traced to its root cause, and fixed. By doing this consistently, we sent a message: ingenuity is appreciated, but we fix what's broken.

"Broken Windows" on the Shop Floor

The Broken Windows theory, introduced by a couple of criminologists in the early 1980s, suggests that when small signs of disorder, like a single broken window, go unrepaired, they signal that neglect is acceptable. Soon, more windows break, and the decay spreads.

Workarounds function the same way. The first "clever fix" may keep production running, but if it's left unaddressed, it spreads. Before long, unofficial processes multiply, data loses credibility, and culture drifts, including safety.

What workarounds are to operations is exactly what broken windows are to neighborhoods: visible signs of neglect that invite more of the same. The longer they linger, the more "normal" they become.

Just like fixing broken windows, you start by cleaning it up. Identify every workaround, no matter how small, find its root cause, and address it quickly. Each one you fix restores order, reinforces standards, and sends a clear message about what the organization values.

The fix: address the workarounds. Celebrate the creativity. But solve the root problem.

"People don't care how much you know until they know how much you care."

This saying, widely attributed to Theodore Roosevelt, is one of our favorites. If people believe you're for them, not just above them, they'll open up about what's broken. That's when real improvement starts.

Take safety. If people think it's only about the recordable rate, they'll go through the motions. When they see it's personal— that you genuinely care—they take it seriously.

Pulse Check: Culture in Action

Do leaders consistently show up, listen, and follow through?

Are workarounds identified and fixed?

When pressure hits, do leaders' decisions reinforce priorities?

Do employees believe leadership cares about them as people?

Culture isn't declared in all-hands meetings or hung on break-room walls. It's built in the small moments—when a leader stops to ask why a workaround exists, when they show up consistently even on hard days, and when they show up simply to check in—to make sure people are doing okay, not just that production is on track. It's built when leaders keep their commitments and follow through on what they say matters.

Those small actions compound. Over time, they build trust, credibility, and stability. When people know what to expect from their leaders—when they see the same authenticity on a tough day as on a good one—they feel safe enough to speak up, take ownership, and stay engaged. That's how culture takes shape: not through declarations, but through dependable, human leadership.

Give them something worth following.

THE LEADERSHIP IMPERATIVE: IT'S YOUR JOB TO HELP THEM GET IT

After visiting dozens of plants across multiple industries, we see a pattern for why some leaders consistently deliver results while others struggle. It's not about luck, resources, or market conditions. The difference lies in how they approach the fundamentals.

High-performing plants share common attributes that distinguish them from those that struggle. Low-performing plants make predictable mistakes that hold them back. The gap isn't subtle; it's obvious once you know what to look for.

If you've made it this far, you already know the central problem: "They just don't get it." Executives don't get operational reality. Employees don't get the business context. Functions work in silos. We all want to win, but misalignment creates frustration instead of results.

Your job is to stand in the middle and connect these gaps. You do that by mastering the fundamentals that separate high performers from everyone else.

Data as The Foundation

High-performing plants: data creates a cadence. Displays reveal what's going on and create a mechanism for urgency and action. Crews know the targets and where they stand against them. They have line of sight and understand how their daily work impacts the business, which creates purpose and ownership. Supervisors aren't chasing random events, only those requiring immediate attention. Managers don't overreact to meaningless signals. The site leader knows teams are aligned and doing what they need to do.

Low-performing plants: everything is both urgent and important, or at least it appears to be. Leaders overreact, often to the wrong things, and get distracted from what is most important. People are frustrated and angry, sometimes to the point of arguments and shouting matches. Without reliable data to separate signal from noise, every problem feels like a crisis.

The difference: high performers use data to create momentum and focus. Low performers live in chaos.

Story-Finding: From Numbers to Action

High-performing plants: leaders don't overwhelm people with charts and graphs disconnected from critical metrics and targets. Real-time displays focus on a handful of metrics people can act on. Projects are scoped and presented in ways tied to pain points the floor understands.

Low-performing plants: even with good data, they overwhelm people with charts that distract from what matters. Information exists but doesn't translate into meaningful action.

The difference: high performers focus information to drive action. Low performers create overload that paralyzes decision-making.

Prioritization: Doing the Right Things Right

High-performing plants: leaders know they can do anything, but not everything. They apply resources to the most important things and finish what they start. There's a cadence to what they do and how they do it. Projects have clear scope, defined timelines, and dedicated resources.

Low-performing plants: leaders keep adding "urgent" projects to the old list. People are spread too thin to do anything well.

The difference: high performers finish by focusing resources. Low performers start but rarely finish.

ROI Thinking: Speaking the Language of Investment

High-performing plants: leaders earn credibility with executives because their projects are focused on business results. That credibility leads to growth, expansion, and promotions. A track record of delivering on promises creates a virtuous cycle of trust and resources.

Low-performing plants: leaders hope for funding for pet projects. When approved, projects often underperform, eroding credibility.

The difference: high performers build credibility through results that match promises. Low performers rely on hope.

Supervisor Effectiveness: Organizational Strength at the Core

High-performing plants: supervisors lead people instead of chasing paperwork. Their time is protected for supervision— daily huddles, in-the-moment coaching, removing obstacles, celebrating wins, developing people. They have time to use the data productively. Role clarity prevents them from becoming the catch-all.

Low-performing plants: supervisors drown in administrative tasks while their teams struggle. Burnout is common; leadership development is nonexistent.

The difference: high performers give supervisors the tools and time to actually supervise.

Department Managers: The Middle That Holds It All Together

High-performing plants: department managers are truly part of the leadership team. They understand strategy and metrics, take ownership for results, and operate as one team. They have each other's backs, share information freely, and show genuine camaraderie. They develop their supervisors and measure success by output and talent growth.

Low-performing plants: managers operate as silos, competing for resources and recognition. Relationships are transactional. They live tactically and reactively, firefighting to hit today's targets even if it creates tomorrow's problems.

The difference: high performers align managers around common goals and mutual accountability. Low performers let departments win while the plant loses.

Partnerships: No One Succeeds Alone

High-performing plants: leaders treat HR and finance as core team members with a real voice. Cross-functional relationships create mutual wins.

Low-performing plants: functions operate in silos with conflicting goals. Decisions are made in isolation; unintended consequences show up later.

The difference: high performers leverage collective intelligence through genuine partnerships.

Culture: What People Actually Experience

The biggest takeaway here is trust.

High-performing plants: Leaders show up with consistency, authenticity, and energy. Actions match words—especially under pressure. Even when decisions are difficult, people trust that leadership is doing the right thing for the right reasons.

Low-performing plants: Leadership presence is inconsistent or reactive. Mixed messages and emotional decision-making create confusion and fear. One day it's calm and collaborative; the next, it's tense and unpredictable. People learn to read moods instead of priorities, to protect themselves instead of improving the process.

The difference: High performers build trust through calm, consistent actions that match their message. Low performers erode it through inconsistency and emotional reactions that shift the focus from performance to self-preservation.

The Reality Check

Moving from low performance to high performance is hard work. You'll face resistance from people who prefer familiar chaos to the discipline of improvement. You'll have setbacks when old habits resurface. You'll make decisions that disappoint some while serving the greater good.

But when you consistently apply these fundamentals, momentum builds. Data-driven decisions create credibility. Solved problems build trust. Effective partnerships multiply impact. Strong shop floor leaders extend leadership. Authentic culture attracts and retains good people.

Your Next Steps

If you recognized your plant in the high-performer descriptions, keep pushing. Excellence is a moving target.

If you saw yourself in low-performer patterns, don't despair. Start with data and build on that foundation. Focus on one chapter's principles until they become habit, then layer on the next.

Remember: you're standing in the middle, between strategy and execution, between executives and employees, between competing priorities and limited resources. It's not comfortable, but it's where transformation happens.

The difference between plants that thrive and those that struggle isn't resources, equipment, technology, or market conditions. It's leadership that bridges gaps, builds alignment, and refuses to accept "they just don't get it" as the permanent state of things.

When you master these fundamentals, you don't just manage operations, you create environments where executives see operational reality in their language, employees see business context in theirs, functions collaborate instead of competing, and you become the conductor, not the fire chief.

ABOUT THE AUTHORS

Don Robb

I've spent more than 30 years in manufacturing leadership, and in that time, I've learned that the real work isn't fixing machines or hitting numbers—it's about building trust, unlocking potential, and creating cultures where people believe they can win.

At RR Donnelley, I had the privilege of leading a nationally recognized open-book management initiative. It wasn't just about teaching people financials—it was about helping teams see how their daily actions moved the business forward. That experience taught me the power of transparency and ownership, and it became a turning point in how I lead.

Later, I took on the challenge of revitalizing an underutilized book manufacturing facility and then then the turnaround at Spectrum Brands' Blacksburg plant. Those experiences weren't easy—both involved tough calls and painful changes—but they showed me how much can happen when leadership, data, and culture align.

Harvard Business Review and Fortune magazine covered some of those stories (see case studies below), but what matters to me isn't the press—it's the people who lived them. The employees who went from skepticism to pride. The leaders who grew in confidence and clarity.

Today, as CEO of Flex-Metrics, I get to take those lessons into dozens of plants across multiple industries. My focus is the same as it's always been: roll up my sleeves, use data as truth, and help leaders build environments where teams thrive and businesses perform.

Bob Siepka

My career in manufacturing spans more than 40 years, and if there's one constant, it's this: the numbers always tell a story, and when you listen, you can transform an entire business.

At RR Donnelley, I led a company-wide productivity initiative we called Operation Compete. By putting data at the center, we uncovered opportunities that ultimately delivered over $80 million in cost savings. (You'll find the full account of Operation Compete in the Case Study section below.) That project taught me how powerful it is when leaders trust the numbers and act with discipline.

Later, at LSC Communications, I managed the world's largest trade book manufacturing facility. It was a complex operation, with big opportunities and big challenges. By digging into the data and working closely with teams, we implemented initiatives that generated more than $1 million in annual productivity and rework cost savings. Beyond the numbers, it was about creating a culture where teams believed improvement was always possible.

Over the years, I've helped lead capital expansions, navigate consolidations, and guide plants through industry shifts. Each transformation reinforced the same lesson: when leaders listen to the story in the data and engage people in the process, the results follow.

Now, as Chief Commercial Officer at Flex-Metrics, I bring that same data-driven approach to manufacturers across industries. My passion is helping leaders see what's possible when they stop guessing, start measuring, and use data as a catalyst for lasting performance.

APPENDIX

Case Study Introduction

The stories you've read are lived experiences that shaped how this book came to be. More importantly, they aren't just our stories. They're lessons learned in real plants, with real people, facing real challenges.

That's why we've included additional case studies in the following pages. These aren't theory or best-practice checklists; they're the hard-won accounts of what it looks like when leadership, data, and culture come together.

You'll see how Operation Compete showed the impact of putting data at the center of decision-making, how open-book management turned financials into a language everyone could use, and how the revitalization of a struggling book plant proved that culture and execution can transform even the toughest situations.

Taken together, these case studies form the bridge between our backgrounds and the practical lessons in this book. They show what's possible when site leaders stand in the gap, bring transparency to the table, and help teams believe they can win.

Operation Compete

In the late 1990s, RR Donnelley faced massive disruption. Digital technologies, the internet, and declining catalog and magazine volumes were eroding demand, but the urgency hadn't fully reached the shop floor.

New CEO Bill Davis stepped into a company where executives felt the financial pressure but couldn't see the operational realities, plant managers knew their facilities but lacked market context, and front-line employees had valuable ideas no one had ever asked for. The challenge was twofold—connect strategy with execution and reduce costs across the network.

Davis brought in McKinsey & Company to deploy their Total Operational Performance Systems (TOPS) methodology—designed not only to cut costs but to break down the organizational walls that kept good ideas buried. The process was deliberately provocative (some said, "ridiculous"): each plant had to identify 40% of its compressible costs, forcing leaders to think well beyond incremental improvements. Over 10 weeks, facilities moved through aggressive target setting, structured brainstorming, risk assessment, and

ABOUT THE AUTHORS | 121

implementation planning—engaging literally every level of the organization.

Bob Siepka stepped into "Operation Compete" at a critical moment—just as McKinsey was phasing out and responsibility for sustaining the process shifted in-house. He inherited a massive, high-visibility project with aggressive cost-reduction targets, deep skepticism from plant leadership, and fear on the shop floor about what the changes might mean for jobs.

Bob built credibility by listening first—acknowledging concerns, clarifying the purpose, and emphasizing that the process would surface operator-led improvements, not just top-down cuts. Yes, it was a corporate mandate, but one that needed exceptional leadership.

He handpicked and trained internal facilitation teams who understood both the methodology and the company's culture. These teams worked side-by-side with plant managers and operators to ensure everyone had a voice in shaping solutions. The bottom-up flow gave operators and front-line staff a structured way to share practical, high-impact ideas—like repositioning equipment to cut material handling time. The top-down flow gave plant managers critical insight into competitive pressures, enabling them to explain the urgency, align teams with strategic objectives, and lead change with context.

The initiative also fostered inter-plant knowledge sharing, with teams transferring proven ideas from plant to plant. And it gave employees the freedom to voice concerns about unintended consequences. This built trust and improved execution. In addition, by clearly defining the supervisor's role as a translator between management intent and operational reality, the process relieved them of administrative overload and allowed them to lead improvement efforts effectively.

The impact was massive: according to Donnelley's 1998 annual report, the initiative was implemented in 29 plants with savings of $2-3 million per plant, with minimal capital investment. This generated a 170-basis point improvement in company-wide gross profit.

Just as importantly, the initiative proved that when strategic vision and operational knowledge are deliberately connected, organizations can achieve results that neither side could deliver alone.

Open-Book Management at RR Donnelley's Northeastern Division

In "Opening the Books" (Harvard Business Review, 1997), John Case introduced the concept of open-book management (OBM), showing how companies that teach employees to understand financial results and connect daily work to profits can transform skepticism into engagement. Rather than telling people what to do, OBM gives them the why, empowering teams to think and act like owners.

Case specifically highlighted the initiative led by Don Robb in Donnelley's Northeastern Division, where he championed open-book practices to involve the entire workforce in understanding and improving the business's performance. Working in partnership with Jack Stack's Great Game of Business coaching group, Robb helped bring the principles of the Great Game—originally proven in smaller entrepreneurial settings—to one of the largest printing companies in the world.

The Donnelley initiative became one of the earliest large-scale applications of OBM, proving that the Great Game could scale beyond small firms to complex, global manufacturing environments. That precedent showed how financial literacy and transparency could drive not only cultural transformation but also significant operational and financial gains.

Revitalizing the Roanoke Book Plant

In "Elite Factories" (Fortune, September 2003), the Roanoke, Virginia, division of R.R. Donnelley was profiled as one of America's top-performing manufacturing plants.

Once a facility facing steep challenges, Roanoke was transformed through a combination of disciplined leadership, workforce engagement, and digital integration. Under the leadership of Don Robb, the plant adopted open-book management principles that gave employees visibility into financial and operational performance, teaching them how daily decisions impacted the bottom line. This transparency and accountability built trust, aligned the plant around shared goals, and helped shift the culture from skepticism to ownership.

By pairing advanced technology with an empowered work-force, Robb and his team repositioned Roanoke as a model of adaptability in a shifting industry. The turnaround not only restored competitiveness but also earned the plant recognition as one of the nation's most admired manufacturing workplaces—demonstrating that large-scale, legacy operations could achieve elite status through openness, rigor, and cultural change.

THE $60-TO-$157 JOURNEY

HOW MARKING SYSTEMS TRANSFORMED MANUFACTURING WITH DATA

The Moment Everything Changed

In 2006, Marking Systems expanded to a 40,000 sq ft facility, making it impossible for Greg Van Beber to oversee operations directly. Initially, they relied on a manual clipboard system to count press impressions—a slow, inaccurate method that fueled guesswork and profit swings. "You may go back there and during that minute, things are flying," Greg said. This guesswork led to frustration and tension between sales and production.

The Unix-to-SQL Miracle

Their transformation began at an EPMS trade show during a move from Unix to a SQL-based ERP. They discovered

Flex-Metrics integrating directly with EPMS, enabling SQL-to-SQL data flow—no manual exports. Flaviu Borcoman, IT Director, built a unique system others struggled to comprehend.

The Day the Operator Finally Got Heard

Operators initially resisted time tracking, causing tension. Greg chose culture over short-term output, sacrificing an hour of production to implement metrics. Data revealed a press issue ignored for weeks by management, leading to repairs and new calibration schedules. Operators saw data as a voice, not punishment.

The Matrix Moment

Flaviu describes early analytics as overwhelming "numbers and numbers" until he could "see the code." Translating data into clear visual dashboards allowed managers to quickly spot issues and make decisions, transforming raw data into actionable insights.

Elephant Hunting: The 40% Swing

"Elephant hunting" found major losses in setup times, operating at 70-80% efficiency. Improvements pushed them beyond 100% to 120% efficiency—a 40% swing. Last month alone, they saved 172 setup hours and 500 overall labor hours, equivalent to three to four jobs eliminated through natural attrition.

The Underdog Champion

Flex Metrics revealed quiet heroes with top performance, leading to promotions and recognition of employees previously overlooked.

The Customer Tour Transformation

Marking Systems impressed customers by showcasing live Flex Metrics dashboards during tours, demonstrating technological leadership and cost transparency, winning respect even when their prices were higher.

The $60 to $157 Transformation

The key metric—shipments per weighted hour—increased from $60 to $157 per hour. Headcount dropped from 123 to 73 through attrition and cross-training, not layoffs. They optimized labor creatively across roles.

The T-Shirt Company Experiment

Applying Flex Metrics in low-margin t-shirt printing created a profitable subsidiary, T-Shirt Tycoon, with 200 employees and $20M in sales—outperforming typical industry profits.

The Meeting That Changed Everything

Monthly manager meetings evolved from validation (scrubbing data) to analysis (trusting data), to optimization (collaborative problem-solving with operators). Real-time display of metrics in production ensured transparency with no surprises.

The Camera Integration Breakthrough

Flaviu recently integrated cameras with Flex Metrics, allowing managers to view exact footage of activities tied to data points, enhancing coaching and accountability.

The Mentorship Promise

Marking Systems offers new Flex customers on-site guidance, sharing best practices to ease adoption, emphasizing culture change over technology acquisition.

The Hard Truth About Success

Flaviu warns, "Don't buy this thinking it will let you do less work." Greg stresses executive commitment as crucial—without leadership pushing through initial resistance, transformation fails.

The Master Class Moment

Flex Metrics' Don Robb called their approach "Master Class leadership," praising the focus and strategic use of the tool.

Looking Forward: More of the Same

Their scalable approach now extends to sales metrics, assembly work, laser cutting, and beyond, building a culture of data-driven decision-making in every corner.

The Bottom Line

Marking Systems went from guesswork to precision, from $60 to $157 shipments per weighted hour, while growing revenue and reducing employees through efficiency gains. Greg sums it up: "I don't like surprises. I want to know ahead of time." This isn't just data—it's transformation.

SUGGESTED READING

Throughout this book, you'll recognize ideas drawn from leaders who shaped the way we think about execution and culture.

Jack Stack's **The Great Game of Business** taught us the power of open-book management and financial literacy on the shop floor.

Stephen M.R. Covey's **The Speed of Trust** underscored that trust isn't a soft skill—it's the foundation of speed, alignment, and results.

John Maxwell's writings reminded us that leadership is influence, not position.

You'll also notice threads of Stephen R. Covey's **The 7 Habits of Highly Effective People**. While we don't always cite it directly, the principles embedded in these habits ("urgent vs.

important," "think win–win," "seek first to understand, then to be understood," and "synergize") run throughout these pages. The 7 Habits became part of our leadership DNA and continue to guide how we translate strategy into action

www.ingramcontent.com/pod-product-compliance
Lightning Source LLC
Chambersburg PA
CBHW040926210326
41597CB00030B/5190